Jeremiah Bonn

How to Analyze and Influence People
Decoding Body Language and human psychology, speed- reading people, unlocking verbal clues, Analyzing Behavior and Personality Types

Copyright @2019 By Jeremiah Bonn

All Rights Reserved.

The following Book is reproduced below with the goal of providing information that is as accurate and as reliable as possible. Regardless, purchasing this Book can be seen as consent to the fact that both the publisher and the author of this book are in no way experts on the topics discussed within, and that any recommendations or suggestions made herein are for entertainment purposes only. Professionals should be consulted as needed before undertaking any of the action endorsed herein.

This declaration is deemed fair and valid by both the American Bar Association and the Committee of Publishers Association and is legally binding throughout the United States.

Furthermore, the transmission, duplication or reproduction of any of the following work, including precise information, will be considered an illegal act, irrespective whether it is done electronically or in print. The legality extends to creating a secondary or tertiary copy of the work or a recorded copy and is only allowed with express written consent of the Publisher. All additional rights are reserved.

The information in the following pages is broadly considered to be a truthful and accurate account of facts, and as such any inattention, use or misuse of the information in question by the reader will render any resulting actions solely under their purview. There are no scenarios in which the publisher or the original author of this work can be in any fashion deemed liable for any hardship or damages that may befall them after undertaking information described herein.

Additionally, the information found on the following pages is intended for informational purposes only and should thus be considered, universal. As befitting its nature, the information presented is without assurance regarding its continued validity or interim quality. Trademarks that mentioned are done without written consent and can in no way be considered an endorsement from the trademark holder.

Contents

Introduction 7

Decoding Body Language: How Body Language Reveals Your Thoughts and Emotions 8

How to Analyze People via Non-Verbal Behaviors of the Arms 22

How to Analyze People via the Non-Verbal Behaviors of the Legs 32

How to Analyze People Via the Non-Verbal Behaviors of the Hands and Palm 42

How to Analyze People Via the Non-Verbal Behaviors of the Face 63

How to Analyze People via the Non-Verbal Behaviors of the Head 71

How to Analyze People Via the Non-Verbal Behaviors of the Eyes 88

How to Analyze People Via the Non-Verbal Behaviors of the Lips 99

Reading People 110

Learn the Difference Between a Real Smile and a Fake Smile 114

Notice the Posture: Do People Hold Their Head High When They Feel Confident? 120

What Happens When You Meet the Opposite Sex? 129

Spatial Zones and Territorial Positions 141

How People Use Body Language in the Workplace 155

Unlocking Verbal Clues 167
How Words Reveal Your Personality 171
The Relationship Between Words and Personality 182
Conclusion 189

Introduction

Humans rely on several forms of non-verbal communication regardless of whether they do this deliberately or not. The ability to extract and decode the thoughts and emotions that have triggered such behaviors can be learned and then used later on to your advantage in this complex and changing world.

To guide you in mastering this skill, this book covers specific body parts and the effects each part has on the conveyed message. Since body language needs to be read while considering the context of situation, the book details how gestures can be interpreted in different ways. Verbal clues that further enhance your understanding of a person's thoughts and emotions are also explained to help you achieve a holistic understanding of the factors that influence effective communication.

Although body language continues to evolve, the underlying principles and key points to consider remain consistent. Thus, in time, you too can be an expert at reading people.

Decoding Body Language: How Body Language Reveals Your Thoughts and Emotions

Though the study of body language has only formally started in the 20th century, early humans have relied on non-verbal cues signaled using different body parts to communicate with one another. Experts in the various fields of study, particularly psychology, social studies, and history, concur that body language, along with the other major components of our non-verbal behaviors, influence day-to-day interactions in ways that we may not even realize in the first place. These wide-reaching effects on the success and failure of our endeavors and relationships have lead researchers to study further how a person's actions and posture can give away their thoughts and emotions.

The human body is capable of creating a wide range of non-verbal gestures and facial expressions. Some actions may have been done with intention, such as clapping the hands in appreciation. Others may be committed without any apparent intention behind it, like when we cross our legs while sitting down. There are also certain gestures and expressions that could be associated with a person's identity due to the frequency of their usage. Non-verbal behaviors vary also, depending on the location and culture of person, but there are key gestures that may be considered as universal since almost everybody interprets them in the same way.

Experts have categorized gestures and expressions as they go along with their studies on the intricacies of body language. These categories can be condensed into the following main types of non-verbal behaviors:

- Involuntary Gestures and Expressions

    Involuntary behaviors are a direct result of the human's fight-or-flight system, which has evolved from the survival tactics that early humans had developed. These behaviors prevent you from acting in any other manner that goes against the system.

For example, whenever a person feels threatened by a situation, they fold their arms in front of the chest to form a protective barrier against the source of their anxiety. If they are sitting down, the person may also cross their legs over one another as a means of attaining some form of comfort or protecting their most vulnerable areas from harm.

- Signature Gestures and Expressions

    A common non-verbal behavior becomes identifiable with a certain person when it is carried out in a particular way that no one or only a few people do. The gesture or expression must also be observed frequently enough that others would start to believe that it is one of the personality quirks of that person.

    Napoleon Bonaparte is known for his signature pose depicted in many portraits painted by various artists. Standing with a hand enclosed inside his waistcoat, Bonaparte's stance gave forth an aura of dominance and pride.

Athletes are also known for developing signature behaviors that acted as their anchor during critical moments in their matches. For example, Rafael Nadal, a gifted tennis player, always tugs the back of his shorts with his hand before serving. The act has been highly publicized that some even began mimicking his gesture in front of him as a not-so-subtle form of mockery inside the court and even inside the locker room.

Recognizing these signature behaviors can help you decode the person's thoughts and emotions. There is a meaning behind their chosen gesture or expression, and when you have mastered reading them, you can find ways to improve your interactions with that person.

If you do want to be remembered by those

around you, developing your own signature pose can make you quite memorable to them.

- Fake Gestures and Expressions

    Any non-verbal gesture or expression can be faked should a person intend to do so. As a matter of fact, the brilliancy of an actor is measured on how well they can convince others of closely alike their fake emotions and actions to real ones. For an average person, faking gestures and expressions is done to deceive others or conceal their true thoughts and feelings. Regardless of the intention, fake non-verbal behaviors can still be identified because key components of the genuine gesture or expression are missing.

    Common examples of gesture and expressions that are usually faked include smiling and crying. A person that appears to be in pain may also be just faking it if they simply adapt the correct facial expressions and act in a slow, stilted manner.

- Micro Gestures and Expressions

    Micro non-verbal behaviors are quick, almost indiscernible flashes of a person's true thoughts and feelings that they would rather keep hidden. These are more frequently observed on the face, such as tiny twitches around the corners of the mouth or the flaring of the nose.

    These micro gestures and expressions are done unintentionally. A person chooses to frown at someone, or wave their hand in goodbye. However, that person cannot keep the tension in their eyes or the tremor in their hand from showing and telling others of how they truly feel at the moment.

- Displacement Gestures and Expressions

    During situations of high stress and pressure, people tend to commit non-verbal behaviors that only serve to release excess energy and tension. These actions do not aim to resolve the situation or complete a certain task. These gestures and expressions merely provide comfort to the person doing it, even if it is for a short moment only.

Common examples of displacement behaviors include stroking the chin with your fingers, tugging at your earlobes, fiddling with other objects, and removing imaginary dirt from your clothes. Lighting up a cigarette, taking a few puffs out of it, and leaving it in the ashtray without finishing the whole stick is another instance of a non-verbal behavior done by some people to alleviate stress and tension. The person doing it may not be really in the mood for a smoke, but they believe that this action may take the mind off from their thoughts and worries.

- Universal Gestures and Expressions

Several key gestures and facial expressions are so prevalent that they are considered to be universal by body language experts. Most of these non-verbal behaviors are rooted in our genetic make-up as human beings, and thus the reason for its widespread usage across the world.

Smiling is foremost facial expression that comes to mind when thinking of universal non-verbal cues. It depicts a positive message from the initiator, though some cultures, such as the Japanese people, use it as well to convey embarrassment.

Though the act requires certain facial muscles to tug up the lips and crinkle the corners of the eyes, it is so effortlessly done that even infants are capable of smiling. Different people may have unique ways of smiling—they may even be faking it—but the general meaning behind this gesture remains the same.

Conversely, people know that when someone cries, they are experiencing profound sadness. Infants are born with a loud cry after having been extracted from the relative comforts and safety of the womb. They have not been taught to do so, but they still cry out at the top of their little lungs.

When a person feels shy or embarrassment, the cheeks redden into what we know as a blush. This is caused by the sudden rush of blood from the chest to the face, and such reaction cannot easily be controlled. Due to the involuntary nature of this non-verbal behavior, it is considered by many as a universal sign of shame.

Shrugging is another universal action that denotes the need of a person to protect themselves from others. When people shrug their shoulders during questioning, they are trying to shield themselves from the possibility of answering incorrectly or giving away information they would rather keep as a secret. The gesture may also be done to indicate indifference to the situation or towards another person.

Though universal non-verbal behaviors exist, gestures and expressions still vary from one culture to another. To become a master at reading other people's thoughts and emotions through body language, it is imperative for you to learn how different cultures commit and interpret gestures and facial expressions. What is acceptable for one may be considered as offensive by others. As such, learning the nuances of non-verbal behaviors for the different cultures around the globe is critical to the success of your interactions and relationships.

Appreciation and valuing the diversity of gestures and expressions is only one key component of becoming a good reader of non-verbal cues. You must be able to learn also the following in order to make use of your full potential as a body language expert.

- Spatial Awareness

    Understanding a person's sense of personal space and territory is vital to achieve balance in how we position ourselves whenever we interact with others. If not, you may end up standing too close for comfort that the other person can even feel your breath fanning up their face. Conversely, you might project to others that you are either uninterested with what they are saying if you stand too far back.

An individual's personal space varies in size, depending on the situation they are in. Where they grow and how they are raised also factors in on how small or large a person's territory is. For example, people from the rural regions prefer a larger personal space compared to those who are originally from cities.

- Anticipation of Movements

    Aside from doing the gesture or expression, understanding the timing of the non-verbal behaviors can also give you an advantage. With this you can anticipate what the other person would do next, or how they will react to a certain incident without needing further information.

    For example, angry people express their violent tendencies in overt manners that make it possible for you to react quickly and avoid being in the receiving end of a punch or a kick. It may also save you from embarrassment during first dates. Others may hesitate about kissing their date's goodnight, but if you know which signs to look for, then you may act accordingly and avoid any further awkward moments with your date.

- Mirroring of Gestures and Expressions

    Anybody can mirror the actions of another person, but it takes a body language expert to do it without making the other person feel like you are mocking them. The objective of matching your behavior with those of another person's is to create rapport between both parties by showing them that you understand how they feel and know what they are thinking of. It connects you to them in a respectful way without making it downright obvious.

    However, if you end up mimicking every movement without thinking about it first, then the person will immediately see through your actions. Mimicry is different from mirroring since the former elicits suspicion from others, while the latter shows support and understanding.

- Responding Appropriately

Reading others' body language is only the first step to a successful interaction and good relationship with others. Observing how they act and express themselves can tell you what they are thinking of and how they are feeling during that moment. Through this, you have gained an insight about their next movements, and a clue on how you should behave and respond.

For example, if your friend hangs her down and wraps her arms in front of her chest, her gestures imply that she needs to be comforted and may appreciate a simple consoling pat of the hand from you. On the other hand, if you notice a frown forming on her face while her body stiffens further, it indicates that you need to leave her alone for the time being.

Learning how to recognize and interpret body

language are helpful skills to acquire, particularly for the career and day-to-day living. It improves the first impression we give to others upon meeting them for the first time. Gesture and facial expressions enhance the words we use by providing illustration or emphasis to our point. In some cases, they can even serve as effective substitutes for speech altogether. Most importantly, it reveals the beliefs, feelings, and dispositions of everyone, including ourselves. By decoding body language, we can get a chance to discover new sides of ourselves that can be corrected or improved upon further.

How to Analyze People via Non-Verbal Behaviors of the Arms

Using the arms as a means of comfort and protection is ingrained into our system. During early childhood, we would cling on to our parents for solace, or hide behind large objects whenever fear strikes. As we grow older, we learn that social situations do not permit such behaviors, so we develop various coping and defensive mechanisms.

One of the most common ones that would be carried on until later in life is the act of crossing our arms in the front, at one side, or at the back. This gesture signifies different meanings depending on the context of the situation, but in general, crossed arms denote apprehension or insecurity due to some perceived threat.

There are some people, however, who do not agree with this observation. They would claim that rather than conveying negative feelings and attitude, folded arms is just another habit with no inherent meaning behind it. They just do it because the gesture feels comfortable. What they fail to realize is that in high-pressure or threatening situations, we seek comfort, and the most natural way to get it is through ourselves. We should also remember that even though the gesture makes us feel better, other people may not see it that way. As previous studies have shown, most people perceive crossed arms as a sign that you are not approachable.

Aside from negatively affecting your impression on others, folding the arms also affects your attitude towards them. An experimental study has exhibited how students who listened with relaxed arms and legs scored higher in terms of retaining information compared to those who were instructed to cross their arms in front of their chests throughout the whole lecture. The researchers have noted that the latter group became more critical of their instructor and paid less attention to the lesson. By simply reminding the students and leaving room for them to uncross their arms, educators can significantly increase the amount of information learned and retained during a class.

To help you decode the meaning behind different forms of crossed arms, here are the important relevant observations gathered by leading researchers on body language.

- Arms in Front of the Chest

    Folding both arms across the chest is recognized as a negative, defensive stance in almost any situation. For example, during rallies held by politicians in front of a live audience, it is a common sight for dissenters to express their sentiments non-verbally by crossing their arms in front of them as they listened on. Good, experienced speakers would immediately notice this cue. They will try to pinpoint the exact moment of disagreement, and aim to recover or alter the attitude of the audience into being more open-minded about their arguments. They may also try to throw in a couple of ice breakers to change the mood.

Continuing your point without addressing this negative non-verbal cue would be a waste of time. Even if the other person has said, in definite words, that they are in agreement with you, their body language would tell you the truth.

Excellent negotiators and salespeople know the most effective ways of getting the other party to uncross their arms. Handing out documents, pens, or brochures is one of the tricks they use to change the negative attitude of their listeners. Another way is to ask for the listener's opinion or input about the subject at hand. This implies that they are open to the ideas of the listener, and that they would like to be granted the same attitude by the listener as well.

- Clenched Fists While Arms Are Crossed

This non-verbal behavior indicates a higher level of defensiveness and agitation. The person may be feeling hostile, especially if the gesture is combined with clenched teeth and redness of the face. To handle this, it is advisable to placate first the person before trying to uncover the reason for their apparent hostility towards you.

- Crossing the Arms and Gripping Them with Hands

    When a person grips both upper arms with their hands, it indicates that they are distressed and in need of comfort. In some cases, the person would grip their arms so hard that their knuckles would turn white from the lack of blood circulation. This non-verbal behavior is commonly seen in a hospital setting, where people wait for updates from medical professionals about themselves or their loved ones. Travelers who would be boarding an airplane for the first time are also observed to be exhibiting this gesture while waiting for their respective flights.

- Partial Crossing of the Arms

In stressful situations, people may attempt to provide comfort to themselves by recreating the feeling of being hugged. This is done by placing one hand on the other arm, forming a protective barrier across the person's front or back. Usually seen among women, this stance indicates insecurity during tense circumstances. For example, introducing yourself in front of a crowd can be quite a nerve-racking experience. People have reported feeling more at ease when they do this gesture while going through the experience.

- Crossing of Hands

Instead of partially crossing their arms, men are more likely to cross their hands in front of them during stressful situations. Researchers believe that this stems from their need to protect their most vulnerable assets from being attacked. In fact, studies show that this behavior has caused men to evolve with shorter arms in terms of their ratio to the rest of the body. This is noted among the likes of male athletes before a game, or men who are about to receive an award in front of a live audience.

- Disguised Arm Barriers

    People may use the objects they are holding or that are around them to conceal their feelings of insecurity or apprehension. For example, drinking from a cup or glass requires only one hand, but a nervous person would use both hands instead. When feeling anxious, a person may arrive for a meeting while holding a folder or clipboard in front of their chest. It may also be in the form of small arm gestures such as adjusting the cuff links during formal events.

    Women have even less subtle ways of expressing their distress. Clutching the handbag close with both hands or close to the sides is a common example of disguised arm barriers.

The act of crossing the arms would always be regarded in a negative light, regardless of its cause or form. It does not only reflect your state of mind, but it could also affect your attitude towards others and vice versa. If you want to project a more positive image of yourself, then avoid relying on this form of defensive mechanism and make a habit out of using open gestures instead.

When we touch ourselves, the act gives other people clues on how we are feeling at the moment. According to experts, self-touching is an unconscious effort to comfort ourselves by mimicking the sensations of being touched by another person—usually our mothers or caretakers. There are various forms of self-touching that shows the nuances of this coping mechanism, but the most common one is hugging oneself whenever we feel stressed out or pressured.

During childhood, most people experience being comforted by a hug from a parent-type figure. Another common way to placate an upset child is to stroke them until they have calmed down. This is why when people grow up, they want to replicate these sensations in order to take the mind off certain stressful situations or recurring insecurities.

Since it might be considered as inappropriate to seek such form of comfort from relative strangers, and not everyone has a close friend or family member that could step in and give the comfort they seek, the best provider for such needs is the person themselves. Common examples of this type of arm gesture include rubbing the hands against the face and neck, and stroking the arms up and down.

Arms are not only used as protective barriers in terms of body language. Open arm gestures are associated with an accepting, friendly, and casual attitude. By positioning your arms wide open, you are showing that you have nothing to hide from other people. In response, people become more drawn to you since they feel more at ease with your approachable demeanor.

Certain cultures also use open arm gestures whenever they express their greetings and farewells. In fact, it is a common sight in the airports to see family members and friend welcoming or bidding their goodbyes to loved ones with heartfelt embrace. Depending on how strong the bond is between the person, this intense gesture may last for a relatively longer time than casual hugs. Curiously, experts have noted that welcoming embrace tend to be longer than those given during departures.

How to Analyze People via the Non-Verbal Behaviors of the Legs

Studies show that people are less aware of their legs and feet in comparison to the rest of the body. In terms of human anatomy, the closer the body part is to the brain, the more conscious we are of its movements. Because of this, we are able to control better our facial expressions compared to the non-verbal cues signaled by our legs and feet. This means that if you want to assess how a person actually feels at a given moment, analyzing the position and movement of the legs and feet could give you a more truthful result.

A series of behavioral experiments has depicted how the lower limbs could be used to identify people who tell lies. Initially, the researchers instructed a group of people to lie in the most convincing manner they could. Most participants tried to control their facial expressions, hand movements, and tone of the voice. However, almost none of them noticed the increased movement in their lower body as they told the lie. Another experiment would validate these findings, and would further elaborate that this explains business executives feel at ease while sitting behind a solid desk since this covers their legs and feet.

Aside from giving away the truth behind our words and expressions, the legs and feet also reflect our feelings and attitude towards other people or in a given situation. For your guidance and reference, here are the meanings behind the common positions and movements of our lower extremities.

- Standing at Attention

    Generally seen in military settings, standing at attention is characterized by keeping both legs and feet close together while facing forward. It shows neither positive nor negative attitude towards the other party, but it could signal that the person they are speaking to is in a higher rank than them. For example, in a workplace setting, employees usually stand at attention when talking to their immediate superior.

- Standing with Legs Apart

   This stance implies dominance and a macho attitude, especially among men. Experts say that the masculine connotation is brought about by lack of regard towards frontal attacks to the genital area—which is one of men's vulnerable points. Regardless of the exact cause, standing with legs apart signals that person will not be leaving any time soon.

- Standing with One Foot Forward

   Historically, placing one foot in front of the other is a popular pose among the rich and famous. This allows them to show off their expensive garments and shoes. Nowadays, standing with one foot forward can be used as a way to understand the current feelings and attitudes of a person.

   Analyzing the direction of foot in front of the

other can show you where the person wants to go or how they feel towards their companions. For example, you can tell a person wants to leave if their foot is pointing towards the direction of the nearest exit. On the other hand, if a person feels attracted to another person within a group, at least one of their feet would be directed towards the latter. When we are interested with the person we are talking to, our subconscious urges us to take a step closer to that person.

- Standing with Legs Crossed

  If standing with legs apart indicates confidence and openness, standing with legs crossed shows insecurity about the situation or lack of familiarity with the people around. For example, if a new employee joins a group conversation among tenured staff, they may feel out of the loop or in worse cases, unwelcome. The new employee might express their anxiety and uncertainty by crossing their legs, and sometimes even their arms as well.

Conversely, if a stranger suddenly stands too close to you while waiting for the bus with your friends, you—and perhaps your friends too—might feel uncomfortable with the perceived threat. Arms or legs will be crossed until either the stranger walks away, or your group boards the bus.

Though there are various forms of sitting with legs crossed all of them denotes negative attitudes and feelings. For example, in a business setting, a boss who sits with legs crossed are more likely to be abrupt in making decisions but less likely to retain information discussed during a meeting. They also tend to be more critical of others, especially when it comes to reviewing proposals. The following explanation on the different types of this posture will elaborate on the subtle variations in the meaning of each.

- Figure Four

    Sitting with a figure four crossed legs requires you to place the lower portion of one leg on top of the thigh or knees of the other leg.

Commonly seen among American men, this posture exudes a combination of competitive and antagonistic disposition. It is also an indicator to avoid asking for a commitment or decision from the person. Studies show that most people finalize their decisions with both feet on the ground instead.

Some women—while wearing trousers or jeans—may also exhibit this posture whenever they feel argumentative. However, they tend to do this in the company of other women only to avoid sending out any unwanted sexual cues or to maintain their feminine appearance.

Another version of the Figure Four style is formed by gripping the crossed leg with one or both hands, essentially locking the person in the position. It has been observed that people who do so are more obstinate when it comes to being faced with information or opinions that are contrary to what they believe in.

- European Style

    Crossing one leg over the other in a neat manner represents the European style of this posture. This does not mean it is limited only to European countries, since it is observed in different cultures around the world.

    Sitting in this form indicates that the person is feeling distant from the other party or the current situation they are in. Trying to coax out an agreement from that person would be hard, if not impossible, since they are not open to communicating at that given moment.

- Locked Ankles

    When someone locks their ankles while sitting down, it signifies their attempt to restrain themselves from verbalizing their thoughts or true feelings. This could out of their lack of self-confidence, niggling doubt, or perhaps a growing sense of dread about the situation they are in. For example, if an applicant is feeling uncertain during a job interview, they might cross their ankles and draw back their feet under the chair they are sitting on in order to hold themselves back from saying something that could be detrimental to their success.

A study on body language conducted among law enforcement officials explains that that people brought in for questioning locked their ankles more often out of fear instead of guilt. In order to get over this, interrogators are required to undergo training on effective questioning techniques that could get ankles unlocked and key information revealed.

- Entwined Legs

Timid people relies on this gesture whenever they feel the need to retreat into themselves. Usually seen among women, locking one foot around the other leg indicates uneasiness, regardless of how relaxed the face expressions or body movements are.

Again, people who claim to do this gesture out of habit do not realize the subconscious trigger in their system. As multiple studies on non-verbal behaviors have concluded, feeling a sense of comfort from gestures like this one is a direct result of negative emotions or attitudes towards the situation or other people.

How a person walks also reflects their current state of mind and emotions. A happy person that appears to be brimming with energy can be seen walking with a bounce on each step. The arms swing high in both directions; Heads held high as if they are marching forward. On the other hand, people who would rather slip back into bed and catch more sleep are observed to be slumping down while they practically drag their feet to reach their next destination.

A person's manner of walking can also be a projection of the image they want others to believe about them. Confidence is expressed through brisk, but long strides that makes the person appear purposeful and self-assured.

Though mostly ignored when a person evaluates the body language expressed by another person, the legs and feet can be revealing if you know which signs to look for. Standing, sitting, or walking, there are various ways to tell how a person feels or thinks about you, an idea, or a situation, even without prodding them to share such personal information with you.

How to Analyze People Via the Non-Verbal Behaviors of the Hands and Palm

The human palm is associated with various meanings ranging from the truth, emotional accessibility, service, and authority. When people want to show that they are not lying or pretending, they put up their hands and display their palms for everyone to see. Therapists who want to reach out to their clients express this by enhancing their words with open hand gestures.

Our palms are one of the most effective body parts in terms of non-verbal communication. Palm gestures can be categorized into the following three main types of positions:

- Palm Facing Up

    By gesturing with your palm facing upwards, you are exhibiting submission towards the other person. From an evolutionary point of view, it proves that you are not carrying or hiding any weapon thereby eliminating the threat that you might be posing initially. It is also similar to the way homeless people seek and beg for alms out in the streets.

For example, if you use this gesture to ask someone to move a box into another location, that person would take this more as a request rather than a command from you. They will not feel obliged to follow your bidding since they feel no pressure to do so.

Another situation wherein this gesture would help is during conversations. By signaling the other person with your palm facing up, you are telling them that you wish to listen from their side as well. This is especially helpful for those who do therapies or counseling as a profession.

Over the years, people have also incorporated this gesture to their needs, but the general meaning remains the same. A good example of this is seen whenever we pay respect to the national flag. People are expected to put their palm over their chest as a sign of deference to the history and achievements of the country.

- Palm Facing Down

    A sense of authority is apparent when someone gestures with their palms facing downwards. Depending on the status of the receiving party, the effect of this gesture varies.

    Following the one of the examples given above, asking some to move a box by gesturing with your palm facing down would provoke different reactions. If the other person is of higher status than you, they are going to be offended about your command. Those who are of equal standing might feel resistance to follow your lead. However, people who rank lower than you would take this as an order since they believe you have the power to do so.

An infamous example of a person who often uses this non-verbal cue is Adolf Hitler. Known as the Nazi salute, this particular palm gesture became a symbol of supremacy and dictatorship during World War II. Nowadays, people tend to avoid using this gesture in case they might be associated with the cruel tendencies that Hitler and the Nazi regime had embodied.

A more typical example involves hand holding. It has been observed that when a couple hold hands, the dominant partner—usually the male—has their palm facing either downward or backward, while the submissive partner receives the gesture with their palm facing upward or forward. This small gesture is indicative about the distribution of power between the couple.

- Palm Closed, Finger Pointed

By pointing a finger with the palm closed, you are signaling the other person that they have to your bidding or else there will be consequences for them. Many cultures all over the worlds finds this as annoying and downright offensive. To avoid making this mistake, some people choose to either use the thumb or the palm facing up position whenever someone asks them for directions.

A research study conducted on the effects of this palm gestures to the listeners is conducted to ascertain how people's perception of the speaker varies depending on the usage of each gesture. Using professors as speakers and university students as the audience, the researches recorded the feedback of the latter after a given lecture.

Among the three gestures, using the palm facing up has yielded the highest rating from the students. This positive feedback dropped significantly when the lecturer used the palm-facing-down position. Least of the three is the pointed finger position, with some students even walking out at some point while in the middle of the lecture.

Aside from getting the worst feedback, finger pointing has also lessened the retention of information among the listeners. Rather than focusing on the content of the lecture, the students began forming personal judgments against the speaker instead. They describe the person using pointed finger gestures as "rude" and "aggressive", despite the speaking of the same content as the other speakers who used the other two types of palm gestures.

If you work in similar settings as this, it is advisable to phase out any tendency to point fingers at your audience. Instead, develop gestures using palm facing up or down to achieve better feedback and increase the learning gained by your listeners. Another good alternative to finger pointing is by done by pressing the tips of your thumb and forefinger to form the universal signal for "okay." According to studies done on this gesture, the feedback about the speaker are generally positive. "Focused" and "thoughtful" are some of the common description given by the listeners about the users of this gesture.

Another common but powerful gesture that differs depending on the position of the palms is the handshake. The use of this non-verbal behavior dates back to our primitive ancestors. Back then, tribes with good relationships between them greet each other by extending out their hands with both palms exposed to show that they mean no harm to each other. During the height of the Roman empire, some people have the habit of concealing their weapons in their sleeves—just in case they need to protect themselves. Because of this, a typical greeting during the Roman times involve grasping each other's wrist or lower arm to check for hidden weapons.

Nowadays, handshakes are used as type of formal greeting or as a means of finalizing an agreement between two persons of similar status. Until recently however, only men shake hands in business settings upon initial contact or before ending the meeting. Due to exposure in the media and continual usage, handshakes can now be expected to be done by both men and women, and during various social contexts.

Across the world, the modern handshake is being adapted even if the culture has already an existing method of greeting other people. For example, the

Japanese people traditionally bow to each other in greeting or as a form of deference. However, handshakes between Japanese businessmen are now becoming more common, especially when they deal with foreign nationalities.

Ideally, initiating a handshake is expected whenever two people meet for the first time. Still, there are some instances wherein this gesture could be construed as inappropriate. For example, pushing for an unannounced meeting with a prospective client just to secure a contract could be damaging for the chances for the salesperson, if not handled well. By initiating a handshake during this situation without any preamble may cause the other party to feel forced and further push them away from the idea that the meeting is beneficial for them as well.

To help you determine whether or not to extend out your hand for a handshake, you may try asking yourself the following questions.

- Is my presence here welcome or not?

- Is my agenda for being here clear to the other person?

- Did I get the timing right for this meeting?

If you answer no to any of those questions, then you will have to explain or apologize first to the other person before asking for a handshake. This will save you from a potential faux-pas that could be detrimental to your actual objectives.

In some countries, women are not allowed to shake hands with other people. Prevalent among Muslim countries, handshakes initiated by women are considered as improper. However, according to a recent survey, women from other countries are now being regarded in a better light when they do firm handshakes as a form of greeting others.

There are several types of handshakes that demonstrate different meanings about the initiator and the recipient. In general, the meaning of a handshake can fall under the following stance: dominance, submission, or equality. Whether intentional or not, the said attitudes will be conveyed to the recipient and can significantly affect the success of the meeting.

- Dominant Handshake

    Your handshake exudes dominance if your palm is facing downwards. It doesn't have to be a full turn; a slight tilt of the hand would have the same effect as long as the recipient has noticed your movement. Doing this type of handshake shows that you are in control, or that you are of a higher status than the other person.

    If you want to counter someone who initiates a handshake with their palm in a downward position, there are two methods that may help you achieve equality or even dominance over the other person. First, you can try stepping closer to the other person using your left foot. When shaking hands, most people normally steps forward with their right foot, thus leaving them almost no room to counteract. By shifting to the left foot first and adding a couple steps more, you will be invading the other person's space and will be in a position to straighten their downward facing palm or even turn it upwards into a submissive position.

The first method seems like an arm-wrestling match and may cause severe discomfort for both parties. If you want to avoid this, you may opt for the second method instead. A double-hand style is not less subtle, but it might be better received by the other person. This is executed by responding first with the palm facing upward and then placing the left hand over the back of the other person's right hand. This position will allow you to change the tilt of the handshake and adjust the balance of power in favor to you.

Though your intention may be good, relying the double-hand style for all situations may be counterintuitive to your initial goals. For many, it is only acceptable to receive a handshake with two hands if both parties have established a good relationship prior to the act itself. Otherwise, if you initiated this gesture upon meeting for the first time, then it would only be seen as an attempt to control the other person, and will make them question your intention. Hence, as a rule, use the double-hand style only when a hug would also be acceptable as a form of greeting or farewell.

- Submissive Handshake

    Conversely, initiating or accepting a handshake with your palm facing upwards indicates that you are letting the other person to be the dominant one instead. This position is typically followed by a soft—or even limp—press of the hand signaling either weakness or insincerity.

    Though this type of handshake is generally seen as a submissive behavior, there are some cases wherein it may be taken as a considerate action. For example, surgeons who rely on the dexterity and integrity of their hands may opt to give a weak handshake instead in order to protect themselves from damage. People suffering from illnesses, like arthritis, may not have any choice but to do a limp handshake since they are physical incapable of doing otherwise.

Some situations also end up with better result if you give a submissive handshake. Shaking hands after an apology will be a more effective gesture if you would submit to the other party.

- Equal Handshake

When neither party manage to turn the handshake into either side, the resulting effect tells that both persons are of equal status to each other. It also shows that the no one is willing to give in easily to the other person, or that they both feel respect to one another. Whichever the case is, this style of handshake ranks as the most effective in creating better rapport and maintaining a positive relationship between the involved parties.

Starting a handshake with a vertical position is not enough however for a handshake to be qualified as an effective gesture. You must also be mindful of the pressure of your hand. Ideally, you should reciprocate with the same amount of force as you have received from the other person. If you are going to shake hands with multiple people in a row, it is advisable for you to adjust the grip of your hands accordingly as well. According to evolutionary studies, men use almost double the amount of pressure than women. Of course, this would still vary depending on individual factors, such as personality and physical countenance, but keeping in mind these guidelines would help you execute the perfect handshake.

Handshakes can be practiced in order for you to achieve the ideal form. It is important to learn the right amount of pressure and the acceptable number of pumps. However, it would also help to know which types of handshake you should avoid at all cost. As you go on, check if your current handshake form belongs to any of the following, and strive to correct the bad points and prevent damages to your credibility.

- Cold and Sweaty

    Known also as the Wet Fish, this handshake is considered as the least appreciated gesture by many people. A damp and sticky hand characterizes this form due to the accumulated sweat on the palm. Oftentimes, the hand also feels cold to touch. For some, this is caused by a genetic condition called hyperhidrosis, which causes them to sweat profusely. This, however, is not enough of an excuse since you can use a handkerchief or tissue to wipe off the excess moisture. It should be noted that hand wiping should only be done before a handshake and never after doing so, since this action would be highly offensive to the other person.

    The general reaction of this gesture's recipients shows that the initiator is seen as weak and insincere. Some people even associate it with the level of commitment of the person to their agreement. According to studies, those who shake hands with cold and sweaty palms are mostly unaware of the said effects. There are also those who are unaware too of the condition of their hands. As such, it would be greatly helpful to point this out and suggest ways to correct it, in case your friend is one of those people.

- Too Strong a Grip

Many businessmen are guilty of using this style of handshake, believing that it makes them appear stronger. They start a handshake with the palm facing down and proceed to pump the other person's hand in a sharp and vigorous manner. Finally, they spend a few seconds gripping the other hand with enough pressure to cease incoming blood flow.

Though normally used as a means of persuasion, there are some who use this style as a pre-emptive move since they feel that the other person would try to dominate the handshake. In either case, this handshake is considered as uncomfortable by the receiving party.

- The Crusher

   This is similar to having too strong a grip, but with more intense force applied to the pressure on the other person's hand. A person with an overly aggressive or enthusiastic disposition is most likely to commit this faux pas.

   Unfortunately, whether or not this gesture is done to intimidate the person, there is no way to counteract before your hand could be crushed. If the situation permits it, you may try to bring other people's attention to the rather violent act, while remaining polite and restrained. This may cause the said person to change their ways and stop it from happening again.

- Grabbing by the Fingertips

Commonly seen when a man and woman shakes hands, this form happens when one grabs the other person's fingers instead of the palm. This is mainly due to the difference of each gender's acceptable personal space. Men generally have smaller allowance than women. So, when a woman stands a little further back when the handshake is initiated, the chance of missing the mark goes higher.

Many people see this as a sign that either or both party lacks self-confidence. It may also indicate that one of them feels uncomfortable about the situation they are in. To recover from this, you may try to use your other hand and place it over the other person's hand enclosed with yours. Then, with a smile, initiate another proper handshake. This would prevent any misguided attempts to correct it, which usually leads to more mistimed handshakes. Doing it over again will also improve your standing with the other person since you have placed importance on getting things right.

- Thrusting Out a Stiff Arm

    Another common trick used by aggressive people is extending out, in a brisk manner, an arm for a handshake. This happens when the person sticks out their hand even if the distance between them and other person is still too far for the arms to bend during a handshake. As a result, the initiator will have to lean forward just to meet the hand of the other person, leading to an unsightly balancing act.

    Studies show that people mainly to this to preserve their sense of personal space. For example, those who are raised in the rural regions are more used to having a larger need for space. Their behavior tends to be more territorial as well, so they would prefer to keep their distance from strangers or even acquaintances.

- Pulling Back an Arm

    Similarly, the act of pulling the other person's

arm into your personal space during a handshake is also considered as improper behavior. Many power players rely on this method, but as research has shown, it only serves to offend the other person and present the initiator in a negative light.

- Too Many Pumps

    Characterized by a series of quick, energetic vertical shakes of the hand, this type goes over the acceptable number of pumps per handshake. According to body language experts, up to seven pumps may be considered as acceptable. Beyond that, it shows overenthusiasm or lack of knowledge about proper decorum on the part of the doer. As such, this is more commonly seen again among those from the rural areas.

    In some cases, the person who pumps too many times may try hold on to the other person even if the pumping had already ceased. This may cause further discomfort on the other person, but it has been observed that only a few people try to get themselves out of this hand lock. Studies show that the physical connection between two people lessens the likelihood of retreat during situations like this.

How to Analyze People Via the Non-Verbal Behaviors of the Face

According to studies, most people would rather believe what they see on another person's face than what is being told to them. Since humans are naturally visual creatures, we rely more on what we can see with our own eyes.

Due to the wide range of emotions that can be reflected through facial expressions, many people find these non-verbal gestures as among the easiest to read and interpret. However, facial expressions may also be faked in order to manipulate or deceive other people. Learning the indicators of each emotion as exhibited through facial expressions is a key skill that must be gained to get an accurate reading of other people.

- Happiness

    Genuine expressions of joy are evidenced by a

set of facial expressions that are signaled by your brain as you feel positive emotions. Since it is an automatic response, attempts to fake this expression are distinguishable to those who pay attention to non-verbal behaviors of other people.

True happiness is displayed across the several facial features. The eyes sparkle as crease lines on the outside corners of the eyes deepen. The rounds of the cheek raise when the lips are pulled up at the sides to form a smile. The person may then either remain smiling or continue to a full-on laughter.

- Sadness

A sad person's expression is characterized by dull and sagging facial features. The eyes appear lifeless as the eyebrows droop down or to the sides. Moisture may accumulate in the lower lids of the eyes, signaling that they might be on the verge of crying.

The mouth may either be pressed together in

a flat line or pulled downwards into a frown. If a sad person wishes to keep others from seeing their state or to block out the cause of their emotions, they may use their hand or an object to cover the face.

- Disgust and Contempt

    Depending on the situation, the following basic expressions of a person experiencing disgust or contempt changes accordingly. Both eyes narrow as the head turns slightly away from the source. The nose wrinkles while the mouth twists into a grimace. People may also either drop or lift slightly their chins in reaction.

    Disgust is typically caused by a foul sensory experience or gaining knowledge of an incident or idea that runs against your personal beliefs or preferences. For example, you may find yourself grimacing and gagging over the smell of unwashed socks after a day at the gym, or flinching away from reports of a violent crime committed by a member of your community.

Contempt, on the other hand, is more frequently seen in business settings. People may throw around expressions of scorn and disdain towards co-workers who annoy them, or towards those who they consider as rivals for a dream position.

- Anger

You can tell if a person if feeling angry by the following set of facial expressions. Their eyebrows are furrowed together as the upper facial muscles pull them down towards the nose. Flared nostrils is also evident, but only for some people. The lips are either pursed or turned downwards into a frown. There may also be tiny movements of their jaws, indicating that they grinding their teeth together. In some cases, the mouth may be opened in a stiff manner, taking an appearing of someone screaming in silence. Lastly, the skin can appear reddish or pale, depending on the level of anger felt by the person. This is due to our natural fight-or-flight instinct, which affects the blood flow to and from the face.

These signs are coupled with sharp movements of the head, body and limbs. The person may also be staring down hard at the trigger of their anger. As such, expressions of anger are easily recognizable to anyone nearby.

- Surprise

According to studies on non-verbal behaviors, humans find it hard to keep their surprise from the showing through facial expressions. When someone is surprised, their face opens up in reaction to the stimuli. Eyebrows arches up and wrinkles in the forehead deepens. The whites of the eyes are displayed as the eyes widen in a quick manner.

Some people even drop their jaws in surprise, giving them a slacked-mouth expression. There are also people who also cover the mouth with their hands to express genuine or fake surprise. This gesture denotes their attempt to restrain themselves after being startled or surprised.

- Fear

A fearful facial expression appears similar to a surprised expression. The differences show depending on how the facial muscles tense up and react. Instead of merely arching up, the eyebrows also furrow together forming more wrinkles on the forehead. Majority of the exposed whites of the eyes are within the upper portion only, since the lower eyelid raises up as well. Lastly, the mouth is left opened when then lips pulled back due to the tension felt by the person.

- Interest

Facial expressions can express interest towards a person, an object, or an idea. If your interest has been piqued during a meeting, your head may turn towards the person and start nodding in agreement. The eyes will widen to absorb more information, while the mouth may part slightly as continue to focus on the what the person is doing or saying.

This expression may vary depending on the nature of the interest we feel—it may be friendly, romantic, spiritual, or intellectual. Regardless of that, the basic gestures indicate openness.

As you become more engaged with observing the other person, your body may begin leaning forward as your face continues to display an expectant expression. You may even begin to raise a hand and place it against your cheek or chin in a thoughtful position. The frequency of succeeding nods is also indicative of the level of interest. Slow nods denote continued immersion and the willingness to listen more, while short, frequent nods tell that while you are in agreement, you want to move on to other matters instead.

The way we express our thoughts and emotions through our face can be influential on the outcome of our interactions with other people. Studies show that, aside from the eyes, the face is the most reliable way to tell how another person truly thinks and feels. The tiny movements involved in the different facial expressions are hard to fake completely so there will always be a single tell that would give away your attempts to fake a facial expression.

Facial expressions are also a convenient way of communicating with others when words do not suffice, or when speaking out loud would be deemed too hurtful or inappropriate. The non-verbal behaviors of the face can also further enhance the potency of a message. With the right facial expressions, a simple lecture can turn into a memorable discourse between the speaker and the listeners.

How to Analyze People via the Non-Verbal Behaviors of the Head

Every tilt and turn of the head can reveal a wide range of emotions and thoughts—from confidence to embarrassment, or happiness to grief. How a person positions their head can also change how others interpret their words or actions. For example, turning the head away can be a sign of submission or an attempt to conceal information.

Even the slightest movement of the head can be used to communicate an order or a request. A person can establish dominance over others by positioning the head in the right way. If not, they may end up displaying arrogance or aggression instead. Given that, it is important to learn what message various head positions convey.

- Superiority

Raising the head to assert dominance is almost an automatic body response since it has been ingrained in our subconscious that this is one of the ways a person of authority acts. According to body language experts, when a person has been announced as a leader, the non-verbal behavior changes to command the attention of others to the power bestowed upon the said person. There are times when a leader would lower their head down for a short moment to show humility, but the head would always revert back to its raised position as the person adapts into the position of power given to them.

Further studies suggest that raising the head can significantly improve the mood of the person. The feelings of superiority associated with this action can alter a person's self-perception for the better. This effect has been observed to people suffering from depression or experiencing high levels of stress and pressure.

- Arrogance

Arrogance may be exhibited when you tilt your head back and thrust forward your chin. Unlike a simple raised head, this position signifies stubbornness coupled with feelings of misplaced superiority.

There are instances, however, when this behavior is used by a person to mask their lack of self-confidence or insecurity about the situation they are in. The distinction can be seen in the angle of the tilted head. An insecure person will tilt their head away from the source of their insecurity, as if trying to get away. By doing so they are putting protective barriers around them, and thereby making this action a defensive posture instead.

- Aggression

When a person is feeling violently angry towards another person or an object, the head tends to be lowered down slightly and thrusted forward from the shoulders, making them look like they are about to charge. The posture makes the person like they are about to engage in a fight by butting their head against the other person or object. If you are on the receiving end of this gesture, it would be wise to stay away from that person so as to avoid any altercation or physical harm.

This non-verbal behavior can also be observed among athletes that play physically taxing sports, such as football and boxing. In such cases, the action is deemed appropriate and even cheered upon by the spectators.

- Disapproval

Much like many other non-verbal behaviors, expressing disapproval through the movements of the head requires other bodily gestures to be effective. There are three general ways a person can show their lack of approval about an idea, object, or action committed by another person.

The first posture involves lowering the head so that the forehead would slant forward. This is combined with a stern gaze directed upwards or towards the direction of the object of their displeasure.

The second posture requires the head to remain still in an upright position. The rest of the face and body has to appear stiff—icy stare directed straight at the other person, both arms folded, and legs crossed if in a sitting position.

The first and second postures rely on a hard gaze to convey the disapproval felt by the person. On the other hand, the third way makes use of a lowered head position that signals a person's silent protest. The gaze is directed down to the ground while the fingers appear to be flicking off imaginary dirt from the person's clothes.

- Rejection

An almost universal way to reject someone or something is through a head shake. According to researchers, this behavior starts as early as the infancy stage of human development. Since babies cannot speak words to indicate their wants and needs, they rely on several non-verbal cues, which includes shaking their head. For example, babies would turn their heads from side to side when they do not want to drink their milk anymore.

As humans grow older, we develop further nuances on this gesture. Generally, there are two meanings to a head shake depending on the speed of the head movement. If your listener shakes their head briskly, it means that they are in disagreement with you and wants to speak out their argument. However, if your listener slowly shakes their head, it indicates that they do not believe what you are saying, but would still like for you to continue speaking.

- Intimidation

Similar to expressing rejection, trying to intimidate someone requires a combination of head and body gestures. To establish an intimidating pose, the head must be thrown back with both hands wrapped around the nape or the back of the head. The elbows stick out as a result of the motion. The chest is puffed out, making the person appear larger than normal.

- Defiance

Defiance is exhibited by also throwing the head back, but immediately followed by small shakes of the head. This signals that the person is not interested with you or has no intention to commit to what is being asked from them.

- Invitation

The head may also be used as a form of attracting attention and inviting someone over to your current position or to follow you to another location. Typically done with a hand, sending out an invitation can also be effective when signaled by the head. This gesture involves throwing the head in a diagonal motion and repeating it over and over again, depending on how insistent you are about the invitation.

- Intimacy

Touching someone else's head denotes that a deep bond exists between you and the other person, or that you have power over the other person. For example, a mother cards her fingers through her daughter's hair, smoothing down the stray strands before she begins braiding the hair. This shows an intimate bond between parent and child. Conversely, a student touching the teacher's head would be an odd sight and would require an explanation on why the action was done in the first place.

Another way of demonstration a special bond between two people is by kissing one person on the head. The kiss signifies affection and protective feelings towards the recipient of the gesture. Again, since this is a one-sided gesture, the initiator of the kiss implies that they have superiority over the other person.

Nodding is almost a universally recognized non-verbal gesture that signals positive messages such as acknowledgment, encouragement, approval, or understanding. Since body language reflects a person's thoughts and feelings, it is safe to assume that a person is in agreement or in a good mood when they nod their head during a conversation.

This gesture is also rather contagious. It has been observed by experts that if a person nods their head at someone else, the gesture is likely to be returned regardless if the other party fully agrees or not. Hence, professionals in different fields, such as sales or psychotherapy, rely on this gesture when pitching to their clients. Here are the various ways on how nodding the head can improve their rate of success.

- Encouragement

Nodding the head is a simple but effective way to achieve a flowing conversation. This non-verbal behavior indicates that the speaker still has the attention of the listener. By doing so, the speaker is encouraged to share more information and talk for a longer period of time.

The speed of the nod, however, is critical since the frequency of the nod denotes other meanings as well. Nodding the head in a rapid motion while listening tells the speaker that even though you are paying attention to what is being said, you want to speak your side as well or that you want to add further information. Slow nods with an even pacing throughout the conversation denotes that you agree to what is being said, but has nothing else to add to the conversation.

If a speaker receives no nods at all during the conversation, they may find it hard to continue. They may be wondering if the listener is even paying attention to them. Thus, the conversation quickly ends from thereon.

- Understanding

The strength of a nod tells the observer if the gesture is a sign of approval or mere understanding. A firm head nod indicates that the person approves, while slight but quick shakes of the head in an up and down fashion denotes that they understand the point being made.

To the naked eye, there seems to be no difference a nod that indicates understanding from a nod that signals a person wants to take over the speaking role. The key in distinguishing these two similar gestures is in the eyes of the listener. If the person maintains their gaze on the speaker while nodding, it means the listener understands and supports the other person. However, if the person nods but looks away, it means they are gearing up to speak instead.

Tilting the head to one side can communicate interest in the person or object that someone is looking at. Men and women differ in the manner they tilt their heads to show interest—Men usually shift their head back to show attention, while women tend to turn their head toward the object of their interest. Regardless of these nuances, the meaning behind the gesture remains the same. A head tilt signals that the attention has been caught and that they are eager to know more.

- Canting the Head

Canting the head is a gesture that beckons the attention of others to the person. It can also be used as an alternative to head nod in signaling that the listener is paying attention to the speaker.

The meaning can also vary depending on the person's gender. Generally, men cant their heads to indicate recognition or acknowledgment. Women, on the other hand, tilt their heads to the side as a form of flirtation or playfulness. The action also makes them appear less guarded and thereby more open to the advances of other people.

According to researchers, canting the head is more commonly seen among women than men. In paintings from the Middle Ages until the Victorian Period, famous women are more frequently featured with their heads canted compared to their male counterparts. As such, the gesture has developed and become associated with feminine means of seduction.

- Cocking the Head

Rather than canting their heads, men are more inclined to cock their heads instead. This involves lowering down their head for quick second before raising their chins up towards the other person. Researchers suggest that this action develops from back in the earlier days when men touch or doff their hats to greet others from afar.

Women may also use this gesture, but rather than a form of casual greeting, they cock their heads to break the ice. This provokes the other person, usually men, to give in to the woman's intention.

According to Charles Darwin, one of the pioneers in the study of evolution, humans bow their head as a sign of submission. The gesture makes the person appear smaller in stature and less threatening.

People bow their heads for two reasons. First, they will do that if the person they are approaching or has approached them is of a higher position than them. In some cultures, the lower the position of the head, the more respect is being shown by the person. Different cultures have their own versions of this gesture. In the UK, people are expected to perform a full curtsey when in the presence of the Queen. The Japanese salespeople, on the other hand, bend even their upper bodies down the middle as an expression of gratitude to their valued customers.

Another reason for bowing the head is to express apologies. For example, some people bow their heads when they walk past two people engaged in a deep conversation as a sign of apology for the inconvenience or intrusion they have caused.

Research also suggests that people touch their own heads or the back of their own neck to provide comfort and relieve stress. It is common to see stressed people trying to cradle their own heads into their folded arms. A person may also sit back and support the back of the neck with their hands. Both gestures are rooted to the time when our own mothers have cradled us to reassure and comfort us.

Resting the head on one head, however, signals that the person is either feeling tired or bored. This gesture also develops from the infancy stage of human development, wherein whenever we feel drowsy, soft touches of the hand would lull us into sleep.

Resting the head on one hand out of boredom also looks similar to the gesture that signifies deep thought. A famous sculpture by Auguste Rodin called "The Thinker" showcases this non-verbal behavior. Though the man featured in this artwork rests his head on one hand, he is also leaning forward in a sitting position.

To differentiate a look of boredom and thought, you must observe the eyes and the energy a person exudes. A bored person has a dull glaze over their eyes and the rest of their body would appear as slacking down. On the other hand, a person caught in their thoughts have eyes that sparkle with interest. The body usually is tense and appears ready for further action. The hand supporting the head may even be stroking the chin with the use of the thumb and forefinger.

Using both hands to hold the head signals a different meaning, too. Clasping the head with both hands denote a person's need to protect themselves from a real or perceived threat. In times of calamity, people are often told to cover their heads and shield it from falling objects or any other form of harm. Hence, when people feel harm is coming their way, the body's natural response is to protect the head at all costs.

Whether we hold our head high or lower it down, the way we position our heads shows others our state of mind at the current moment. They can take over or even be more effective than spoken words in telling others of our wants and needs. As such, distinguishing the meaning a certain head position holds will always remain a vital component to the study of body language.

How to Analyze People Via the Non-Verbal Behaviors of the Eyes

Comfortably holding the gaze of another person is the key to be more effective in communicating your intention and achieving your objective. This gesture promotes trust between the two parties and inspires confidence in your abilities. However, keeping their gaze can be uncomfortable as well, especially if your instinct is telling you that other person may dishonest or unreliable. The ease to how well you can establish and maintain eye contact depends on the intensity and duration of the gaze, as well as the tiny facial and body movements that happen during the eye contact. Because of these, the meaning of a held gaze changes accordingly.

- Showing Interest

    When someone fixes their gaze directly on another person or an object and holds it there for slightly longer than what they normally do, it denotes that interest has been sparked within the said person. According to studies, looking at a person for more than three seconds indicate interest and signals permission or want for the other person to look back as well.

- Creating Rapport

  Once you have expressed interest, building rapport can also be achieved through eye contact. By holding their gaze for at least 60% of the time you have spent together, the likelihood of improving the bond increases as well.

- Building Intimacy

  If you find the other person attractive, eye contact can also improve your chances of creating an intimate atmosphere between you and the other person. Letting your eyes wander down the face and below the chin level indicates that your level of interest extends beyond casual or friendly. If the other person reciprocates the gesture, then your attempt has been met with a positive feedback. If not, then refrain from doing so again as this will ruin your relationship with the other person.

- Showing Dominance

    People of authority or high status exhibits their dominance over others in various non-verbal gestures including eye contact. Since they aim to exude self-confidence, their eye movements tend to more deliberate and smooth. They feel no qualms about looking at other people, but still remains mindful to not overdo it since it would them appear angry or rude instead.

According to studies, people avoid or break eye contact due to either feelings of discomfort or as a sign of submission. Our basic survival instinct tells us to flee whenever we feel threat, but this is not an option for many modern-day occurrences. As such, humans have developed another means of self-preservation during situations where they would rather run away instead.

There are also some contexts wherein avoiding or breaking eye contact may be seen as a seductive gesture. In the end, the meaning of action depends on the intention behind these gestures.

- Flicking Eye Movements

    When a person's eyes move away from you to another area, it indicates that they are subconsciously searching for ways to escape from the conversation. Even though their head remains still, eyes that move across the room means that they would rather be somewhere else. They just want to keep this from you so that they can reposition themselves when an opportunity presents itself.

- Glancing Sideways

    Depending on the situation, a glance to the side can mean interest, doubt, or hostility.

Looking at someone from the corner of your eye will indicate interest if you add in a smile and raised eyebrows. This gesture is mostly used by women to show they find others as attractive or interesting.

- Dropping the Gaze

    The act of looking down instead of meeting someone else's gaze can either be a sign of submission towards the other person, or a way to keep feelings and thoughts hidden. It is also seen as gesture of reluctance, wherein the person would rather leave than engage in a conversation or interaction.

    However, body language experts concur that if this behavior is done on with a deliberate intention to make the other person feel in control, it could be considered as a manipulative tactic. This method works for those who wish to gain something without outright demanding or pleading for their needs and wants.

Other eye movements that denote various meanings are winking and blinking. Winking involves closing and opening again only one eye, while blinking requires both eyes to be opened and closed. Winking is normally a deliberate action, unless dirt somehow got into one of your eyes—it then becomes an automatic body reaction to the foreign object. On the other hand, blinking is an automatic and necessary bodily movement since this keeps our eyes from drying out.

For many, winking is playful gesture that is associated with friendliness and fun activities. If you wink after saying or doing something, it tells others that your words or actions should not be taken too seriously. It has also been popularized in the media as a signal of two people being in on a secret.

Blinking, on the other hand, is not associated with these light-hearted connotations. According to studies, the rate of eye blinks depends on a person's current thoughts and feelings, as well as the activities they are doing at the same moment.

- Longer Duration of Blinks

Humans blink an average of seven times per minute. If someone blinks less than that because they close their eyes longer than they typically do, it means that they need to shut everything out for moment. This need arises due to various reasons, many people find this behavior to be offensive and disconcerting.

Some do it because they are not interested with the other person or their surroundings. It can also be a means of taking a pause to think and focus on the topic at hand. According to researchers, people do this when they are trying to accomplish too many things all at once. To avoid being seen in a negative light when answering a question that you have not anticipated, you may consider pausing first to think while keeping your gaze on the other person. Reorganize your thoughts as quickly as possible, and then speak out your response. Experts say that by doing so, you will achieve a more positive feedback from the other person than by shutting your eyes while talking to them.

- Blinking Too Many Times

The blinking rate is affected by various factors within or outside a person's control. When engaging in exciting or vigorous activities, such as participating in party games or running a marathon, the human eyes tend to blink by around five times more than usual. This is an automatic response of the body to the additional stimuli.

On the other hand, a person experiencing a high-pressure situation also exhibits more frequent eye blinks. For example, former US president Richard Nixon has been observed to blink more often when asked questions he didn't want to answer during the investigation caused by the Watergate scandal. Some liars do know this common signal that could give them away, so they would lessen their blinks instead to further mask their deception.

It should be noted that blinking too many times does not always indicate that a person is lying or going to lie. Experiencing stress after a whole day's work can also induce frequent eye blinks, and this effect does not suggest anything other than that the person is in need of rest and relaxation.

- Blinking Less Than Usual

    Slow blinks are more often associated to feelings of boredom and indifference. A person observed to be blinking less than they normally do is not keen to continue listening to what you have to say, or has no particular interest in the activity they are currently doing. This action is usually coupled by a dull glazed look in their eyes since blinking less causes the eyes to dry out.

    The blinking rate also decreases when a person is feeling hostile. Angry people tend to focus an intense gaze on the source of their negative emotions. This can be a prelude to a major blow-out if the person is not pacified.

Our eyebrows are also observed to communicate signals non-verbally to other people. During ancient times, some forms of greeting are accompanied by rapidly moving the eyebrows up and down. Even our close genetic relatives—both monkeys and apes—demonstrate recognition and express their greetings by flashing their eyebrows. Because of its universality, an eyebrow flash nowadays is considered as a basic non-verbal gesture of acknowledgment.

Eyebrow flashing can also have different meanings other than recognition. When people agree with what is being said by others, the eyebrows may be raised up and lowered down instead of nodding their heads.

Some reserved cultures, however, limits this behavior to be done only when the situation permits it. For example, Japanese people avoid flashing their eyebrows to strangers since it implies sexual interest to the receiving party.

Another eye movement that has sexual or romantic connotation is the fluttering of the eyelids. This behavior is characterized by irregular, tiny movements—similar to a trembling motion—of the upper lids of the eyes. It is more commonly seen among women as a flirty gesture towards the person they are attracted. Sometime, a flickering eyelid does not mean anything at all as well. If a dirt gets into your eyes, then any movement made by the eyelids are meaningless since this is an automatic reaction of the body.

Since majority of our interaction with other people involves looking at one another, the non-verbal signals sent out through the movements of the eyes can be quite revealing. Furthermore, body language expert concur that the eyes reflect a person's thoughts and feelings more accurately than any other body part. Many muscles used to express these signals react to stimuli on an instinctive level, so faking the eye movements can be hard or even impossible. Hence, learning the different meanings behind each non-verbal behavior of the eyes can be a huge step in mastering the science of reading other people through body language.

How to Analyze People Via the Non-Verbal Behaviors of the Lips

The lips are made of a network of nerves and muscles that run over, under, and around the mouth. Since these work independently of each other, each tiny twist or turn of our lips can alter the non-verbal signals we give communicate to others. One side may be turned up as if you are smiling, but then the other side would be turned down into a displeased frown. The upper lips may also be tightened up without causing any apparent movement in the lower lips. Conversely, the lower lips may shake out of fear without causing any movement on the upper lip.

The different muscles controlling our lips can also push forward or pull back the lips. This may cause changes in position of the chin, which can either make you look like you are uncertain about something or displeased about someone.

The tension of our lips can be a deliberate or unconscious act. Regardless, the lips are an effective way of telling how others are feeling at the moment. The different positions the lips can take mean differently.

- Tightening of Lips

    When people hold back their emotion, the lips tend to tighten up due to the tension. It does not necessarily indicate negative emotions such as anger, sadness, or fear. People experiencing sexual arousal also tighten their lips in anticipation.

    The popular expression "keep a stiff upper lip" is derived from the typical English disposition of holding back their emotions especially when out in the public. This phrase originated back during the height of the British Empire and has been carried on until the modern era. The gesture is a means of preserving one's dignity when facing adversity or loss.

Though it can make a person appear brave, the act of maintain a stiff upper lip can also affect the likability of the person. The tight lips indicate concealed emotions, but for some, it may also mean that the person is hiding information. As such, others will begin questioning the motives and actions of the said person.

- Slacked Lips

  When people feel relaxed or sad, the lips may begin to hang loose due to lack of tension. The muscles holding up the lips in a certain position lose their form thereby leaving the mouth appear unguarded. Depending on the situation, slacked lips can mean the person has been fully immersed in their relaxation activity, or that they have given up entirely out of grief or depression.

- Chewing on Lips

  According to studies, people chew on their lips whenever they feel worried or threatened.

From the researchers' point of view, this is a subconscious act of seeking the comfort from the breast of our mothers again. The lips may be the most accessible object to chew on, but this gesture bears similar meaning as to when people chew on the ends of their pencil or the tips of the fingers. Even if a person chooses to chew on their lower lip, upper lip, or both, the meaning behind this action remains the same.

Aside from anxiety, a person may also chew their lips out of embarrassment or self-restraint. For example, during a confrontation, a person would chew on their lips to keep themselves from blurting out something might come to regret later on.

- Pouted Lips

The meaning of pouted lips can denote a wide range of emotions and thoughts. People pout their lips when they feel sad, frustrated, uncertain, or even when sexually aroused. Regardless of the meaning, a pout appears the same to an onlooker. It involves muscle contractions on the chin and the side muscles of the mouth. Both lips press together as the tongue is raised to the roof of the mouth. It may sound complicated, but the action can be performed effortlessly. Even small children have the ability to pout their lips with relative ease.

To differentiate the meaning of a meaning, you have to consider the other facial expressions done at the same time. A person is pouting in displeasure when head is lowered down, creases appeared on the forehead, and the eyes are narrowed. If the lower lip is jutted out as well, it may signal an incoming bout of tantrum.

From an evolutionary point of view, smiling can be seen as a survival tactic developed to assess whether or not someone will be a threat. Back in the early days of man, the need to communicate from far away is vital for the success of their mission. As such, they use smiling to signal an approaching person to tell that they mean no harm to others.

Nowadays, a smile serves various purposes depending on the intent behind it and the context of the situation. This variation results in the following types of smile that a person can put on to express themselves.

- Full Smile

    A full-blown smile involves the most facial muscles among all types of smiles. The muscles encircling the eyes crinkle as the lips are stretched sideward exposing the teeth. The position holds together as the head tilts back slightly. This movement indicates that the person is experiencing high levels of pleasure and pride.

- Tight-Lipped Smile

    This is achieved by stretching the lips sideward, forming a straight line while keeping the teeth concealed behind the lips. Studies show that this smile makes the person appear mysterious, as if they are holding themselves back from revealing a secret. It also makes a person appear more restrained, and could even be read as a sign of rejection among women.

The tight-lipped smile is also a common sight in photos taken of businessmen whenever they are interviewed for a magazine feature on their success. Those entrepreneurs would usually just talk about the general concepts behind their achievements, but never the exact steps they have taken along the way. They are willing to share their knowledge and experience with the rest of the world, but only to a certain extent.

- Jaw-Dropped Smile

    This type of smile involves lowering down the jaw to varying degrees in order to express happiness and enjoyment. Many people see this as a playful gesture, but it may also be viewed as an exaggeration, depending on the context of situation.

Some politicians, such as former US president Bill Clinton, have incorporated this expression into their arsenal of vote-winning gestures. The jaw-dropped smile is also common among several pop culture icons, such as Ronald McDonald of the McDonald's fast-food chain and The Joker, a villainous character that originated from the DC comic book series.

- Smirk

Smirking may be construed as either a sign of self-satisfaction, disdain or cheekiness depending on the intent behind it and situation the person is in. It looks similar to a tight-lipped smile, but the difference lies on the signals each type of smile gives to the receiving party. Instead of appearing mysterious, a person with a smirk is immediately seen as either smug, ingratiating, or scornful.

Culture and social norms also affect the perceived meaning of a smirk. People from the southern states of America generally smile more frequently than the rest of the nation. Hence, they find the smirk as a positive gesture that exudes warmth and friendliness. On the hand, people from the Northern states would find this gesture as suspicious behavior.

- Smiling While Looking Up to the Side

    Tilting slightly your head down while keeping your eyes directed to the other person makes your smile appear coy and youthful. More women use this type of smile so many view this as a feminine gesture. It elicits parental sentiments from men, triggering them to feel the need to protect and care for the other person. It may also be considered by some men as a seductive gesture, indicating that the woman is responding positively to his romantic or sexual overtures.

The late Princess of Wales, Diana, is known for smiling in this manner, which only served to heighten her popularity among the general population. She managed to evoke empathy since the gesture made her appear more innocent and somewhat vulnerable. Her son, Prince William, has also been captured in photographs bearing a similar smile to his mother's—a gesture that made him appear more charming and boyish to the public.

- Sarcastic Smile

    When a smile displays different emotions from each side of the face, it denotes that the person is being sarcastic. This means that the while the expression on one side of the face indicates a typical happy expression—raised eyebrows, a corner of the mouth pulled upwards—the other side shows a displeased frown.

Laughing and smiles are associated together since they denote similar emotions and thoughts. There are different types of laughter depending on how the person brings forth the sights and sounds. Some people laughs from the bottom of their bellies and burst forth without much thought. Others laugh from the chest and the sound is expelled in short bits of air pushing through the nose like a trumpet. The lack of sound may be similar to the act of smiling, except that the shoulders also shake as you try to contain the sound.

Whichever manner a person laughs, the intensity and duration of the laughter indicates the mood of the person. A person who laughs without a care in the world is open about their feelings and does not mind how others would view them.

There are times when laughter would be deemed as an inappropriate behavior. For example, attending a ceremony at the church requires you to remain silent and composed in order to preserve the solemnity of the occasion. Making a joke and inciting laughter from others will be considered as incredibly rude and inappropriate by many.

Reading People

The first step to reading other people through their body language is by noticing their gestures and facial expressions. This may sound quite obvious, and yet many fail to pay enough attention to the non-verbal signals given off by other people. Such instances lead to situations that may have been avoided had they only known what and where to look out for.

Only when you observe can you start understanding what non-verbal behaviors mean. However, this step takes extra care and deliberation from your part in order to be completely successful. An expert in body language knows for a fact that one action does not convey the full message.

Similar to spoken words, people communicate non-verbally through a set or string of gestures and facial expressions that relay what a person thinks or feels at the moment. A single gesture is not the summary of its parts. A smile may mean differently if you had taken note of the movement of the eyes.

Context is also an important factor to consider when reading other people through their non-verbal behaviors. For instance, a person scratching their nose may indicate he is feeling guilty about something, but sometimes a scratch is just a scratch. However, if you did notice other signs of deception like shifting gaze or tense shoulders, then there is high chance that the person is indeed hiding something from you.

You must also observe how people's action relate to what they are saying as well. Inconsistencies between what is being said and what is truly felt may be revealed through body language. Due to the involuntary and usually uncontrollable movements of the body in reaction to an emotion or stimuli, our actions do speak louder than our words.

A common example of such cases occur during arguments between two people. Both of you verbally agree to stop and move on to more important things. However, if you notice that the other person has crossed their arms over their chests, both hands clenched tight as the eyes narrowed into slits, it may suggest that person is far from the idea of accepting the truce. There may be negative feelings that still needs to be addressed in order to achieve closure. If they attempt to catch your gaze, then be ready for another bout of disagreement. However, if they avoid looking at you, then it is not the right time to confront them about any lingering issues between the two of you.

Once you have considered all the factors, the next key component on gaining the ability to read other people is forming the right conclusion based on your knowledge and observations. Known as gesture clusters, our non-verbal actions are usually committed as a group or sequence of body movements that shows the underlying thoughts and feelings we have.

For example, happiness is not only exhibited through facial expressions. A happy person also moves their limbs in more carefree and open positions. On the other hand, someone who has been frightened can be observed with their entire body tensing up and even flinching away from the source of their fear.

Understanding how each gesture affects the meaning

of a person's actions is key to gaining a better understanding of their personality, wants, and needs. You must now learn the various gesture clusters and their corresponding meanings. From there on, you will discover how body language further changes depending on the situation that a person is in.

Learn the Difference Between a Real Smile and a Fake Smile

According to studies, most people are not capable to immediately distinguish a genuine smile from a fake one. Further studies show that the majority does not care because they are already content about the fact that other people are smiling at them. However, since smiling increases a person's likability and persuasiveness, many have associated this gesture with lying.

To test this, Paul Ekman conducted a research on the frequency of smiles given when a person is lying. The results demonstrated that due to the said assumption, the liars—mostly men—keep themselves from smiling at all. If ever they do, the fake smile formed quicker and stayed on longer than a genuine smile did.

There are people who can detect a fake smile quicker

than most. These individuals possess higher levels of empathy or the ability to relate to the feelings of another person. Nowadays, this is also indicative of person's emotional intelligence, a characteristic that is becoming more valuable not only in real life but also for career growth and opportunities.

Learning which signs to look out for will help you identify a genuine smile from a fake one, regardless of how empathetic you are. A genuine smile occurs is an automatic human response whenever they feel happiness. Involuntary movements such as this can be tough to replicate, hence identification of the general indicators of a fake smile.

- More Pronounced on One Side of the Face

    Fake smiles appear asymmetrical because of how brain send signals to corresponding facial muscles. Since this is a conscious effort, the person tries to compensate for the falsehood. The brain then sends stronger signals, but since only one side of the brain is directly responsible for our facial expressions, an imbalance inevitably occurs. The attempt ends up with a stiff, lopsided grin that reveals the difference between the real and the fake smile.

- Lack of Eye Movement

    When people are smiling out of happiness, several eyes muscles move in accordance to the felt emotion. The absence or even the over-exaggeration of these movements indicate an attempt to fake a smile.

    Creases in the outer corners of the eyes appear when a smile is authentic. Known also as "crow's feet", the presence of these lines cannot be controlled or restrained by a person since the involved eye muscles have received the signals sent out by the brain.

    The muscles controlling the raising and lowering of eyebrows are also affected whenever an authentic smile appears on a person's face. When prompted by the signals sent out by the brain, the eyebrows go down slightly towards the eyelids.

If they do not make an appearance at all, then it indicates that only the muscles in the lower portion of the face are at work. Only the lips are expressing the supposed happy feeling of the person. If such an expression is observed, then the person is attempting to disguise their true feelings with a fake smile.

In some cases, a person faking a smile overcompensates for their deception by forcing their eyes to open much wider than necessary. In contrast, the eyes may either be closed fully or partially closed when the smile is genuine.

- Lack of Movement on the Cheeks

    Similar to eyes, cheeks instinctively rise up when genuine happiness is felt by the person. However, unlike the eyes, most people are aware of how their cheeks move when faking a smile, so there is moderately high chance that the person can adjust accordingly and fake this movement as well.

- Lips Forming a Straight Line

    When a person smiles for other reasons other than real happiness or excitement, the lips do not form the expected curved upward lip. Instead, the lips are stretched across the face in an attempt to mimic the natural movements associated with a genuine smile. An example of a straight-lipped that does not denote happiness is one that is drawn out by a feeling of smugness.

- Appearance of Bottom Row of Teeth

    Unless a person has a large mouth that naturally shows both rows of teeth whenever they move their lips, flashing the bottom portion of the teeth during a smile indicates that the person is trying to deceive others with a fake smile. The exaggerated version of the smile is a form of overcompensation for the lack of happiness felt by the person.

    To assess whether or not a person is faking this, observe and pay attention to their habits and past behaviors. Look also for other signs of a fake smile in order to fully verify the authenticity of the smile.

Detecting a fake smile from a real one requires keen observation skills not just on one aspect of a person's face, but rather on the whole facial expression shown by the person. A person may fake their smile for a number of reasons. Not everyone, however, do it for the sake of convincing others of their lie. It may be as a form of self-protection, or as a way to protect other people's feelings from being hurt. Regardless of the reason, a fake smile is always a sign that a person wants to hide something from prying eyes. It is now up to you if you want to respect their privacy, or to further assess what is behind their attempt to conceal their true thoughts and feelings.

Notice the Posture: Do People Hold Their Head High When They Feel Confident?

The right body language is key to projecting a confident image and even getting yourself to believe that you are naturally a self-possessed individual. Walking into the room with your head held high isn't enough, however, to convey this message. You need to learn the full array of gestures, posture and facial expressions that confident people typically embodies. By doing so, you can tell for yourself if a person is genuinely self-assured or just someone who is faking it.

- Assertive Posture

    Good posture is not only beneficial to your health, but also to how other people perceive you. Maintaining an assertive posture can make you appear confident and open to communicating in a constructive manner. This is achieved by keeping each leg aligned with the shoulders. The distance between your feet should be no less than 5 centimeters or 4 inches, but no wider than 15 centimeters or 6 inches. Standing in this posture will allow your weight to be evenly distributed, giving you a more even stance. Shoulders should be leaned back but not in a way that makes you look stand-offish—just enough to make your chest puff out slightly.

It will be helpful to your image too if you direct your feet towards the person you are speaking to in order to show that you are interested and receptive towards their thoughts and feelings. Avoid shuffling your weight from one foot to another since this may be taken as a sign of hesitation or boredom by the other person.

When you are almost always in a sitting position when interacting with your peers or colleagues, you may still practice good posture to appear more confident. Keep your back straight and let the rear part rest on the back of the chair. The feet should still be planted on the floor, even when the other person cannot see it. This simple act can boost the confidence level since it emulates the assertive standing posture. Sitting in this manner will prevent you also from getting a stiff neck or back pains, making you more comfortable throughout the day.

- Eye Contact

    When you hold your head high, it is important to still keep it on a level that will allow you to establish eye contact with the other person. Eye contact implies that a person is open and is not trying to hold back anything. If eye contact is not established or sustained, then the other person may think that there is something else going on aside from what is being overtly said in the given moment. It may also be a sign of submissiveness towards the other person.

Blinking less or giving a person a hard stare is not also a good habit since it will make you appear aggressive instead. The other people will feel uncomfortable rather than assured of your credibility and reputation.

- Appropriate Facial Expression

    A person's default facial expression varies, and some appear to be naturally severe even when they are not feeling particularly upset or angry. This may be sending out signals that are counterintuitive to the image you are trying to project. Even if you have the right posture, if you are not aware of the expressions your face is making, then the success of your interactions with other people will be negatively affected as well.

    Simply practicing in front of a mirror and observing the movements in our face are not enough for you to gather the points for improvement. Ask for feedback from your friends and family, and listen to how they feel they talk to you in a casual setting. From there, you can adjust your facial expressions accordingly.

- Hand Gestures

    The right hand gestures can spell the difference between a confident person and a domineering individual. Pointing the fingers towards another person will never be regarded in a positive way, in terms of effectively communicating with the use of body language. Jabbing your fingers at someone else makes you appear aggressive and intimidating. Even if you are only trying to make a point, this gesture will elicit negative reactions and leave a bad impression to the person being pointed at or those who are witnessing the act.

    Instead of using pointed fingers, practice open-palm hand gestures. Keeping the fingers together while gesturing towards a person or explaining an idea makes you appear professional instead. It also promotes a sense of cooperation as well improves your trustworthiness to the eyes of other people.

When necessary, a firm handshake is expected from a confident person. Limp handshakes should be avoided at all costs since this will not only show a lack of confidence, but will also make others doubt the sincerity of the greeting or agreement made.

It may also be tempting to shove a hand or both hands into the pockets or your clothes, especially if you want to hide the fact that they are trembling. However, comforting yourself through this means is a definite sign for others that you are not as confident as you are trying to appear to be.

Placing the hands on the hips, on the other hand, is not advisable for those who want to project an air of confidence. For most people, doing this stance implies superiority that borders on arrogance. It may also denote impatience for some people.

Crossing the arms in front of the body is not also a recommended hand gesture for appearing confident to other people. Placing an arm barrier between you and the rest of the world shows that you feeling defensive, distant, or uncomfortable.

Lastly, small hand movements, such as fidgeting with your clothes or clicking the pen repeatedly, are not associated with confidence. Instead, these tiny gestures are indicative of the person's level of anxiety during a given moment.

- Still Legs and Feet

    Similar to fidgeting objects with the hand, tapping the foot against the floor while standing is another sign that a person lacks self-confidence. Aside from letting in on others to your true emotions, these repeated, tiny movements can also distract other people from the message you are trying to convey. If you are guilty of relying on these subtle forms of defense mechanisms, you can try correcting them by being aware first of what triggers them in the first place. From there, you can gradually phase them out until you can restrain yourself from making these movements whenever you feel nervous in front of another person.

- Large, Even Steps

    Projecting confidence while walking can be achieved if you take longer strides in an even pacing. Moving too fast may be a sign of nerves or impatience, while moving too slowly indicates a lack of interest or a gloomy disposition. People who move with purpose and authority are regarded as self-assured individuals.

Since non-verbal behaviors give away majority of your true thoughts and feelings, it is vital to master them in order to control the image that you want to project to others. Learning and understanding the meaning behind each gesture will also enable you to identify important cues to look out for in certain situations, such as negotiations or public speaking.

What Happens When You Meet the Opposite Sex?

Experts agree that romantic interest between opposite sexes is best conveyed with body language. It has also been observed that it is physically impossible to restrain our gestures or facial expressions when flirting. Oftentimes, it is also better to express ourselves non-verbally in romantic situations, especially when speaking might ruin the mood or the impression you are trying to create.

Romantic non-verbal behaviors can be intentional or unconsciously done. Regardless of it nature, these gestures indicate that you want to attract someone's attention and show that you are in mood for a bit of romance.

When someone spots a person that they are attracted to, a gesture cluster called the courting signals happen. The stomach flattens as it gets sucked in, whether or not it is needed to be in a better shape. The body posture straightens up and the muscle tones become more noticeable. If walking, the steps become livelier and faster. The eyes dilate, which is a surefire way of telling if someone is attracted to you since this movement is uncontrollable.

There are differences on how each sex proceeds from thereon. Men tend to thrust their chins up as they stand taller. Their chests expand to exhibit dominance and lack of regard for possible harm. Women express their femininity by tilting their heads to side and flicking their hair. They have also been observed to expose vulnerable areas of their bodies, such as the neck, as a show of submissiveness.

Research, however, shows that women are more likely to make the first move during romantic encounters. Around 90% of women initiate the flirting when they are interested with someone. Their signals are subtle though, so as to make the men think that they are still taking the lead when in fact, men are just following what the women has started.

Women's subtlety can lead to their signals being misinterpreted by men, according to studies. Due to higher levels of testosterone in their system, men mistake friendly gestures for romantic ones. This is why men become confused when women shut down their romantic or sexual overtures.

To get better at the flirting with the opposite sex, learning the five stages of courting may help you assess whether the interest of the person on you is romantic or just plain friendly.

1. Eye Contact

    Looking away the partying crowd, Mary spots a man standing alone in front of the bar. She finds him attractive so she keeps her gaze on him for at least three seconds before looking away again. The man notices the budding interest on him. He waits for another sign that the gaze did not occur only by chance. Mary decides to at the guy at least one more time to confirm her attraction. When she did, the man catches her gaze on him. He glances down to check out her body before his eyes narrows and locks with Mary's again. They hold their gazes at each for longer than usual, showing mutual attraction with one another.

2. Smile

   Mary gains the courage to flash him a quick smile or two. The subtlety of the grin implies that she is interested in taking things further between them. If the smile is not returned or if there is no other positive feedback at all, Mary will feel rejected and will decide to turn her attention elsewhere.

   Fortunately, the man is attracted to Mary as well. He raises his chin slightly and directs a smile back to Mary. This is a sign that he wants to pursue this interaction with the current subject of his interest.

3. Preen

   The body muscles of both Mary and the man grows tense as they draw closer to one another. Mary tries to enhance her physical attributes by straightening her body posture. If she is sitting down at the moment, she may consider crossing her legs demurely to show them off, provided that she regards them as one of her best assets. If she is standing, she may adjust the distribution of her weight, thereby shifting angle of her hips to one side of the body. In either case, she may likely tilt her head to the and subtly expose her neck. Her fingers may be twirling around strands of her hair. She may even find herself licking her lips with her tongue. If she is feeling a bit anxious, she might try adjusting her clothes and accessories even though they are not out of place.

On the other side of the courting process, the man adjusts his posture as well to exhibit dominance and vitality. He might take in a deep breath to pull his stomach in and push his chest out. If he feels his nerves growing too, he may run his fingers through his hair, and adjust his clothing or watch as well.

4. Talk

Even though Mary is the first to show attraction, the man will appear like he initiated the conversation by approaching Mary and introducing himself as Robert. Mary does not feel the need to initiate the conversation herself since she has already given earlier the signals that Robert needed to determine the authenticity of her interest towards him.

Robert starts up the conversation by giving a couple of pick-up lines, which might be received positively or negatively by Mary. Navigating through a conversation with a relative stranger can be tough. However, there are a couple of body language indicators that might help prevent any awkward or painful encounters with the opposite sex.

- o If Mary expresses signs of boredom or growing disinterest after a few minutes, Robert may consider walking away to lessen the blow to his self-confidence. Examples of common signs to look out for includes yawning, frowning, and faking a smile.

- o In case Robert discovers during conversation that he had somehow misread the signal given by Mary, then he may try switching gears from romantic to friendly instead. This will prevent Robert being turned down hard for unsolicited romantic advances.

5. Touch

    If during the course of the conversation, Mary realizes that her interest is still captured by Robert, then she will try to find ways to touch him. This impulse may be carried out as if she had brushed Robert's arm by accident, or as if she is only trying to flick off a lint off his shirt.

These stages of courting may not be evident during real-life situations, but experts agree that everyone who has successfully flirted with someone has gone through them. If any of these stages have been missed, then the courting will stop or end up as a failed attempt.

As illustrated in the five stages of courting, men and

women have different ways of expressing romantic interest towards the opposite sex. However, their main objectives for such gestures are one and the same: to increase their sex appeal and attractiveness.

Women highlight their femininity by arching their backs and leaning forward. Tossing the head back while flicking the hair is another common trick that women use to make themselves more appealing to the opposite sex. On the other hand, canting the head to expose the neck makes them appear more innocent and vulnerable—qualities that call onto the men's natural instinct to protect and care. Lowering the head can also be an effective tactic in attracting the attention of men. It makes a woman appear smaller, but her eyes somehow appear wider when she looks up to the subject of their attraction.

Some women also tend to bring their arms closer together to push the breast out and make the cleavage appear deeper. They also pout or wet their lips with their tongue as a show of their demureness and mystique. It also denotes that the attraction felt borders on sexual, which usually intensifies the interest given back by the men.

Women have a tendency to touch themselves whenever their flirt with the opposite sex. A woman may touch her own body parts, usually the throat or the thighs, to signal to the man that she is open to being touched by him in the same manner should the courting be successful between them. Furthermore, touching a body part draws the attention of men to that area. Such action elicits thoughts among men about how it would feel like if they were the ones touching the women.

Typically, self-touching is an unconscious behavior done out of attraction to the opposite sex. However, women who have become aware of the potency of such actions can become experts at calling the attention of men they find as attractive.

Other than touching themselves, women have also been observed to stroke their handbags in a teasing manner in front of the opposite sex. In addition, if a woman feels comfortable with the company of a man, she will place the handbag closer to him, reflecting the trust and intimacy between the two of them. Experts suggest that since a handbag is essentially functions as an extension of the woman's body, allowing others to see or touch it implies a growing bond between the two persons.

On the other hand, men do not employ as many courtship signals as women do. In most cases, men tend to rely on their personal status, wealth, and power to draw the attention of women to them.

In fact, men are all about embodying a textbook alpha male whenever they feel attracted to the opposite sex. They want to appear larger and taller than the people around them, especially compared to the women they are interested in. Their hands may be shoved inside their pockets, or their fingers may be hooked on the belt loops of their pants—gestures that both subtly direct the attention to their crotch areas.

A common sign of attraction that both men and women exhibit are dilated pupils. This is an involuntary response of the eyes whenever we are looking at something that we find as desirable. Since this movement is impossible to control at will, many people take this as definite sign the person they are attracted to feels the same way as they do.

Unless you want to be perceived as an "easy catch" or as an overly aggressive person, practicing muted gestures is advisable for both genders during the early stage of courting. If not, the opposite sex might be turned off from pursuing deeper relationships beyond initial attraction.

To nurture a successful courtship into a full-on romance, there are various ways that a couple may consider doing.

- Mirroring Each Other

    One of the ways to build rapport and emotional bond with another person is through mirroring their appearances, actions, and expressions. Researchers have observed that the closer the couple is, the more matching their behaviors are. This is a result of the empathy felt between the two people, wherein the emotions felt by one person is well understood by their partner.

- Exhibiting Behaviors That Show Togetherness

For many, physical closeness implies emotional closeness as well. This means that if a man and woman hold hands while walking, people tend to assume that they are in a relationship already.

Furthermore, actions that subtly show possessiveness are also taken as a sign of deeper romance that has already went past the initial stages of attraction. A woman straightening the necktie of her husband is showing to those who are watching them that they belong together.

Spatial Zones and Territorial Positions

By instinct, humans form spatial zones around them thereby determining what is comfortable and what is too close for comfort. These zones range from standing so close that you are already touching other people to standing so far back that no touching can be carried out at all. Certain rules also apply to each zones, telling others what the acceptable and expected behaviors are for each. These rules are signaled through body movements that indicate which zone the other person can occupy.

There are five spatial zones, according to the experts on proxemics or the study of how the concept of space affects human behavior. Typically, the relationship between two people determines which zone would be applicable for a particular interaction. Though influenced by cultural and societal standards, the spatial zones can still be categorized as follows:

- Close Intimate

    This zone is within touching distance of no more than 15 centimeters or 6 inches from the person. Individuals allowed in this zone are the person's romantic partner, close friends, and close family relatives. Allowed gestures within this zone are the most intimate and personal of all zones, such as kissing and hugging.

- Intimate

    Individuals allowed to stay within 45 centimeters or 18 inches from the person, but not less than 15 centimeters or 6 inches are still considered as especially close to the person. If not engaging in acts that promote the special bond between two people, those allowed in the Close Intimate Zone usually stay within this area instead since it is more comfortable for both parties. If a stranger or someone you don't particularly like broke through into this zone, the body instinctively turns into a defensive position in order to protect yourself from the intrusion.

- Personal

    Everyone's personal space varies, but on an average, this zone ranges from 45 centimeters to 1.2 meters, or 18 inches to 4 feet, away from the person. Many people from the West believes that this is the ideal space to have a conversation with another person. Taking a step further back can be off-putting for both parties and may end the conversation prematurely.

- Social

    Engaging with others in a business and trade setting requires you to stand within 1.2 to 2.6 meters or 4 to 12 feet away from the person, in order to maintain an optimal level of comfort. If the salesperson assisting you opted to get closer to you than this, you may end up thinking that they are being too familiar with you. Conversely, if they stand further back, you would think that they are not interested in helping you, or even that they being downright rude to you.

- Public

    The optimal distance between you and the crowd—especially when you are going to give a formal speech to an audience—is around 3.6 meters or 12 feet away from you. Positioning them closer will be detrimental to your comfort while making the speech, while positioning them further away might prevent you from making a connection with them.

Aside from the five spatial zones, experts have also identified the following territorial positions that humans maintain in their day to day lives.

- Inner Space

    Only our personal thoughts and feelings occupy this space. Introverted people frequently indulge themselves in this area, while the extraverts retreat back into this space whenever the occasional need for alone time arises.

People who favors this space prefer to keep to themselves. They do still interact with other people, but they tend to be selective about who they will spend their time with and how that will be spent.

- Immediate Outer Space

    This space is where we allow friends, family, and romantic partners to interact with us. Co-workers who have grown close to us are also allowed to be within this space.

- Public Space

    Everybody else that do not fall under the categories mentioned above are expected to stay only in the public space. People who love to entertain others in social settings, on the other hand, may blur the lines between the immediate outer space and public space.

The bigger the personality a person has, the more

space they need to fully express themselves. They use large, overt body movements, like extending out their arms to the sides before hugging another person in greeting. On the other hand, people with quieter personalities prefer small movements, and may even avoid doing unnecessary body movements at all.

By understanding the effects of space on our non-verbal behaviors, you can assess the meaning behind a person's action depending on how near or far you are from their territories and personal space. In general, how a person regards space indicates the following attitudes:

- Ownership

    Touching another person or an object denote that you are in control and that you actually have proprietorship on them. For example, a man guiding a woman to the location of their reserved seats is exhibiting dominance and ownership when he did so by placing a hand on her back. This gesture shows others that the woman was his date and no one else's. Similarly, touching an object suggests that you own or, at least, want to own that object.

- Submission

    Upon arriving at your colleague's house for a dinner party, you do not immediately plop down the nearest couch to sit back and relax. Unless a close personal relationship has been established prior to the party, you typically wait for an invitation to sit. Even then you will try to refrain from touching any object or moving around to check out the interiors of the house. This shows that you respect the owner of the house, and submits to their control over this environment.

- Safeguarding

    Aside from trying to impose control over someone else, humans also tend to safeguard the space that surround them by using different forms of barriers. It may be visible barriers, such as holding a folder close to your chest as you talk to a colleague, or it may also be invisible barriers such as avoiding eye contact with the other person.

Following societal standards, people are expected to respect another person's space and territory. They stay within the allowed zone and limit their behaviors to what may be considered as acceptable. However, on certain instances, some people may ignore these standards and break through the inner zones. If you are not being threatened with physical harm, you may signal your discomfort instead through body language. Arm barriers, for example, are the go-to gestures of people who are feeling uncomfortable during a conversation.

- Level of Comfort

    How you position yourself in terms of angle and distance from the other person also indicates the level of comfort you are feeling at the moment. When among friends, you are likely to stay close and lean towards them. If stuck in an awkward conversation, you might take a step back and angle yourself away from the person.

Turning the shoulders also indicate your attitude towards other people. It tells others that you want to keep your distance from them. Furthermore, turning your back on others is a definite sign that you want to shut them out completely.

While out in the public, there are instances where you cannot avoid being intruded upon by strangers. Going home by riding a crowded bus will expose your arms, shoulders, torso, and legs to direct contact with other people. It will be considered rude if you try to push them away, despite the distress it may be causing you. However, if those touches come closer to any more intimate parts of the body, people will react accordingly by getting away immediately from the offending party, regardless of how crowded the space is.

How people occupy space and how they arrange themselves while in a sitting position reflect their feelings and attitudes about others, thereby affecting the outcome of their interactions as well. This is why establishing the seating arrangement for social events is a vital task that must be accomplished by the host to ensure the success of their activity. Where you assign someone to be seated down shows how you regard them in terms of their status and importance to you.

Sitting around a rectangular table allows people to share a side with equal space allocation, except for those seated at the two narrower ends of the table. People assigned to sit down at the head of the table indicates that they are of a higher status or more dominant than the rest. Square tables, on the other hand, are less formal and more appropriate for brief but direct conversations. If you aim to eliminate inequality of power distribution, using a round table is more befitting for such goal.

Given these, you have to consider first the outcome you want to achieve before seating yourself or assigning seats for others.

- Casual and Friendly Conversation

Sitting down together near the corners of a table promote a relaxed setting for a conversation. There is enough space for both of you to express yourselves with non-verbal gestures, and you can establish direct eye contact with one another. The presence of the table can be a barrier in case the need for it arises, but with the equal division of table space, you are showing that both parties are of similar status.

- Promote Cooperation

When working together while sitting down, people tend to sit side by side. Aside for being ergonomically sound, the position allows you to look at the other person easily as well as mirror each other's gestures in the presence of a third party. The image this projects is a team that works with the same goal in mind and thinks along the same lines. It is important, however, to maintain the expected distance between you and your partner so as to avoid making them feel uncomfortable by your intrusion to their personal space.

- Confrontation and Defense

    Sitting down across one another with a table in between is the right setting when you wish to take a stand and defend your point. The table serves as a barrier, but also sets up a hostile environment where a confrontation may occur. During such cases, a person may further shield themselves from the attack by crossing their arms in front of their chest, or avoiding the hard gaze directed at them.

    The context of the situation, however, should be considered. In social settings, this seating arrangement is taken as positive since it promotes conversation. Reprimanding a subordinate in a work setting, on the other hand, works best if done while you are sitting on the other side of the table to remind them of your authority over them.

- Lessen the Talking

If you want to avoid small talk or if you want to prevent two people from interacting while sitting down on the same table, sitting across but on the opposite diagonal ends would do the trick. This is commonly seen among those who share tables in the library. By using this position, you are implying indifference or even hostility towards others.

- Create Equality

Picking a round table rather than a rectangular or square table can lessen barrier and create an atmosphere of equality among those who are seated around it. However, this works only if no leader has been pre-determined or identified. In such cases, the effect of the round table diminishes.

For example, in the famous Round Table of King Arthur, he positioned his knights around him to signify their equal power and importance to the kingdom. However, King Arthur also belongs to the same table, thus making those who were seated next to him on both sides appear more powerful than the others. The farther away a knight is from the King, the less power he appeared to possess. The one seated across the King, on the other hand, indicated that he might be in a competitive level with King Arthur himself.

Our choice of table for business and family use also reflects the atmosphere we want to create. For official business meetings, rectangular tables are positioned in a U-shaped arrangement to promote open discussions. If used by family for dining purposes, a rectangular table shows that the family is traditional and the members seated at the ends of the table typically make the rules in that house.

How People Use Body Language in the Workplace

From the moment you are interviewed for a job up to your last day in that company, the people around you will be watching how you act within the workplace. Depending on the image you want to project unto them, you can adjust your behavior accordingly if you understand how body language affect their perception of you as their boss, subordinate, or colleague.

First Impressions Last

Being interviewed means that you have to be on your best behavior right from the moment of first contact. People in charge of recruitment and hiring begin making their judgments from how you groom yourself to the quality of clothes you have chosen to wear. With the addition of your gestures and facial expressions—especially the handshake—an applicant has only less than seven seconds to make a great, lasting impression on the interviewer.

Preparing for an interview involves not only reviewing the important knowledge that you must possess about the job you are applying for, but it also entails psyching up yourself to get your mind in the right track. You must also arm yourself with the following key gesture clusters to get you through an interview successfully.

- Making an Entrance

    When entering the office or an interview room, it is important to project confidence right from the start. How you move will influence how others treat you as an applicant. Furthermore, demonstrating confidence indicates that you are a level-headed individual, even within someone else's territory.

    To be perceived positively, a person should take moderately long strides in brisk pace to enter the building or room. Greeting the receptionist or interviewer with sincere smile would always help, especially when this is followed by an expression of gratitude for being given an opportunity to apply for the job.

- Handshake

    Upon entering, an applicant should hold out an arm for a handshake with the interviewer. Instead of doing it across each other over a desk, going around and meeting the person half-way can ensure that the handshake would not end up as a failed attempt by either or both parties. While shaking hands, quick introductions should be made by the applicant and the interviewer.

- Sitting Down

    An applicant may only sit down once prompted by the interviewer. Doing so before being cued may leave a bad impression about the lack of professionalism and common courtesy of the applicant.

    When asked to sit down, the ideal sitting position is achieved by angling around 45 degrees from the interviewer. Face-to-face positions can make the applicant appear like a child who is called in for a reprimanding by the principal.

Respecting each other's personal space is necessary to achieve a better outcome. In general, men move closer to the opposite sex whenever they speak, while women tend to back away. However, it is important to remember that in terms of spatial zones, being in an interview requires a strict adherence to the expected distance between you and a stranger. If the interview progresses well, then it may be considered as acceptable to lean in closer as indication of engagement. However, moving closer too soon by misreading the signals can lessen the chances of landing the job.

- Making an Exit

    When the interview reaches its end, the interviewee can make a lasting impression by smiling again as another handshake is initiated with the interviewer. Expressing gratitude for the time spent by the interviewer in assessing the skills and qualifications of the interviewee can further increase the likelihood of getting the job.

Ideally, the last image an applicant should leave the interviewer is their face. However, backing out of the room would be weird. To achieve this in a more acceptable manner, the applicant can leave the room normally, but then they should pause by the door, look back to the interviewer, and smile once more.

If an applicant has successfully landed the job, it is now up to their work ethics—and acumen in navigating the office politics—to determine the rate of how quickly they will rise up through the ranks. Once of these tricks used to show power in the workplace is through the choice of seats.

As a general rule, it is advisable to avoid seats that can make you appear insignificant and uncomfortable. An example of such seats are those that make you look up just so you could face the other person. This will also force you to expose your neck area to others, which may imply that you are accepting the submissive role.

Learning the key factors to check when choosing where and how to sit down can influence the success of interactions within a workplace.

- Chair with High Backs

    Back then, kings and queens favored high-back chairs for their thrones and even for their seats used when dining alone or in the presence of others. This form reflects their high status in the society. As such, high-ranking officers and employees prefer high-backed office chairs for the same reasons.

    Chairs that feature high backs also offer support to the back of the person, which thereby makes the person feel and appear more at ease. These can also give an impression of having protective shields surrounding the person. Typically, high-back chairs are also made of higher quality materials and fabrics, which only further elevates the perceived status of the person sitting on it.

- Chair with Casters

    Office chairs nowadays usually include casters to improve mobility and usability of these seats. A person that chooses to sit down in this type of chairs show that they want to appear more agile in the workplace. They give an impression of high energy as well unlike those who are seated in fixed chairs.

    The manner of sitting down in a chair with casters while the arms, legs, and back are resting against the chair is usually observed among those who are in charge. Hence, this reclined position denotes authority instead of disinterest or disregard within the workplace.

In terms of negotiating as part of your work, using the right body language can spell the difference between success and failure. Experts suggest that to win in negotiations, one must appear, act, and sound like a winner already. To achieve such stance and mannerism, here are the key characteristics of a successful negotiator.

- Claims Their Rightful Territory

    The right way to start negotiations is by marking your territory. This implies that you are in control and that you have the right to be there. It tells others that you are responsible for your own actions and the consequences thereafter. Most importantly, claiming your territory elicits respect from the other party since you are essentially demanding them to take you seriously.

    To successfully claim a space, a person must use smooth gestures while maintaining an upright posture. The proper amount of eye contact must be established and maintained from thereon. Open gestures also indicate that you have a positive outlook for the outcome of the upcoming negotiations.

- Self-Assured

A self-assured person shows purpose in their every action. Interest is reflected in the eyes as the gaze remains clear and focused on the task at hand. The body posture indicates that the person is alert and ready for action when needed. Their facial expressions show engagement with the other person. All of these are combined in order to create an air of confidence around the person who is about to enter and conclude a negotiation successfully.

- Shows No Unnecessary Movements

Unnecessary movements indicate high levels of anxiety, which could be a disaster during negotiations if made known to the other party. Gestures that are associated with nervousness includes scratching the head or other body parts, and fiddling with clothes or nearby objects.

Exhibiting anxiety through these tiny movements can spell trouble for the other person as well. Studies suggest that when exposed to clear signs of distress, humans are prone to empathize and feel similarly with the anxious person. Therefore, if you show signs that your nerves are getting the better of you, then there is a chance that the other person will be feeling the same way too by the end of your negotiations.

To phase out these types of gestures, it is helpful to develop replacements for them that are not outwardly known as signs of anxiety. For example, carrying a mug full of hot beverage into a negotiation can prevent you from scratching at your face whenever you feel the nerves building up. Pause for a bit and take a sip instead. This way, you are projecting thoughtfulness instead of anxiousness.

Taking a stand for yourself within a workplace also requires a comprehensive knowledge of which non-verbal behaviors you should employ in such situations. To show that you know what you are talking about and that you stand firm on your values and beliefs, maintaining the right body posture is the primary body language component that you should work on.

Planting both feet on the ground while keeping the weight distributed in evenly fashion for both sides of the body can be an effective way of demanding respect from others. This makes a person appear confident and prepared for the arguments that are coming his way. Standing in this manner also encourages other people to listen to what you have to say since you seem to know well the matter that is up for discussion at the given moment. However, staying still for too long in this position can also make a person appear severe and stubborn, so like most things, balance is key to getting the most out of this body language trick.

In terms of a workplace's hierarchy, the higher you are, the more expectations are going to be placed on you. With the increased prospects and challenges, you will have to be more focused yet more restrained in your actions so as to protect the image you have to maintain as part of the leadership team. Those who belong in the C-level offices are never prances around while at work. Staff members will lose respect if their leaders are not walking the talk by behaving poorly instead of being role models to them. Therefore, to achieve success in the workplace using body language, self-awareness is one of the key abilities that must be learned by heart.

Unlocking Verbal Clues

Mastering the science of reading people cannot be achieved by just learning how to recognize and interpret body language, but it should also cover the various verbal clues people give whenever they speak. Effective leaders know that their message can only be fully conveyed if they could say it well with the proper gestures and facial expressions. Such mindfulness in their words and actions show how important it is to learn how our speaking preferences and choice of words reveal our personality to others.

Verbal communication pertains to the words we use to speak out our thoughts and feelings. On the other hand, the ·manner of speaking those words—including the tone of voice, speed and rhythm of speech—are considered as non-verbal clues. Research suggests that only a small fraction of how we truly think and feel are reflected by our words. Majority of our inner thoughts and emotions are conveyed through body language, especially with those exhibited by the face and arms.

Still, for most people, a person's choice of words significantly affects the first impression they leave on others. For example, a person who speaks using informal language during a business presentation will be viewed as unprofessional and unprepared by the listeners. Much like body language, context is important for verbal communication.

The choice of words also reflects a person's needs, wants, and insecurities, even when their intention for speaking out differs from the perceived meaning. A simple joke about a friend's height can indicate a person's feelings of superiority or even insecurity about their own height.

The pronoun "I" can be indicative of an individual's power over other people. Similarly, using the pronoun "we"—especially when you are a part of a couple or a group—creates a positive atmosphere of familiarity and confidence. The pronoun "you" can be a negative indicator, however, since it denotes blame and the lack of accountability of the speaker when paired with emotive words.

To further illustrate this point, studies show that

couples who use more frequently "we" statements are believed by others to be enjoying a longer and more satisfying relationship. During couple's counseling sessions, participants that use "we" when discussing marital disagreements end up with better results compared to those that rely on "you" statements. Experts suggest that "you" and its other forms—such as "your" and "yourself"—negates the effectiveness of the counseling session since the couple typically ends up accusing one another for their past mistakes and recurring unresolved issues.

Differences in gender and age are also reflected by the verbal clues given by a person. Research studies in linguistics suggest that women are more likely to use pronouns than men when referring to other people. On the other hand, men are observed to use bigger words and more prepositions than their female counterparts. As people grow older, they gradually talk less about themselves. Their choice of words starts to lean toward those with positive meanings than negative ones.

Cultural boundaries also affect verbal clues. People

from the western cultures are more likely to refer to words that indicate their individuality, while those from the eastern cultures use words that lessen the impact of their message, especially when it shows assertiveness or aggressiveness.

The status of the person is also indicated through verbal clues. A study found out that in a room of people, the person with higher status in terms of power tend to use less of the pronoun "I" than the rest, provided that the said person has a high level of self-confidence as well. Those from a higher social class are also less likely to use emotion-laden words than those from the lower social classes.

Furthermore, verbal clues are enhanced when paired with the right gesture or body language. When used frequently, it becomes our preferred style of communication. Therefore, to unlock verbal clues, it is imperative for you to consider the person's body language as they speak. This will allow you to gain a better insight on how their mind works and how they truly feel.

How Words Reveal Your Personality

Being mindful of your words and actions means that you care about how others perceive you and how others will be affected by your thoughts and feelings. Through years of observation, researchers have identified several key components in verbal communication and body language that are associated to the following types of personalities:

- Assertive

    A person with an assertive personality is open and honest about their needs, wants, and feelings. When they communicate with others, they are not aiming to gain anything through underhanded means nor impose their superiority over others. They also do not readily submit to the will of another person without evaluating first the intent behind it and the effects of their decision. By doing so, their relationships with other people are strengthened, and problems encountered are more effectively resolved.

The key word that an assertive person uses when communicating with others is the pronoun "I". For example, when you feel disappointment over the lack of progress on a project, you can say, "I feel disappointed when I get no substantial updates about our project. I believe constant monitoring is necessary for our group's success on this." Such a statement shows that you are responsible for your own feelings and thoughts and that you are not blaming your group mate. By saying this, the listener may take your words in a more positive and constructive light.

Instead of ordering people around, they request from the other person for what they need or what. The questions they ask probe also what the other person might need from them, and how others are feeling at a given moment. When rejecting a request or an idea, they let down a person in a respectful way.

Reflecting an assertive personality through your words also require the corresponding non-verbal behaviors expected from a self-assured person. The person's voice is well-modulated, and the words are spoken in clear and calm manner. The body posture is relaxed, while gestures are more open in nature. Their facial expressions show interest and sincerity in their thoughts. They listen well without interrupting the other person when speaking in turn.

- Aggressive

An aggressive form of communication is characterized by words that denote a lack of regard and respect for the feelings and wishes of other people. This stems from an aggressive personality wherein the person is solely focused on protecting their own interests usually at the expense of their people around them. This is achieved by forcing their will to others and suppressing anything or anyone that might pose as an opposition to them.

An aggressive person is observed to use the word "you" frequently when making their demands to others. "You always submit your work beyond the due date" is an example statement of an aggressive person made to colleague. In contrast, a more positive tone for the same message may be like this, "I need you to submit your work on time."

Leaders who rely on the "you" statements are typically perceived as obstinate and egoistical by their subordinates. They command others to their bidding instead of requesting for support or assistance on handling a matter. They rarely ask others questions, unless their goal is to intimidate others. Hence, aggressive people are not effective listeners as well. When denied, they feel bad about the rejection and will work on overturning the decision made against them.

Other factors that indicate an aggressive personality aside from their choice of words may be read through the person's non-verbal behaviors. The voice is louder than necessary, and a demanding tone is taken whenever they spoke of their ideas, needs, and wants. The listener may feel overwhelmed by their domineering body posture and hard gazes. They have low tolerance for frustration so their hands gestures are stiff and even stilted at times. If their frustration continues to grow, they tend to interrupt other people, especially when the topic goes against their beliefs.

- Passive

A passive person does not feel the need or does not have the guts to stand up for their own needs, wants, thoughts, and feelings, when doing so is needed or expected from the said person. They may be lacking this urge to speak out for themselves in consideration of other people's feelings and perception about them, or they could simply be meek by nature.

Passive persons express themselves in words that are have apologetic or submissive tone. They rarely ask for requests or help from others, even when they really need it at a given moment. On the other hand, when others ask something from them, they have a hard time saying no or at least making a compromise with the other person to make it a win-win situation for both parties.

Their body language also reflects their submissive and restrained personality. They tend to avoid making eye contact with other people. They are frequently observed to slumping down, while their facial expressions and limb movements indicate that they are holding back their true thoughts and feelings about a certain matter.

- Passive-Aggressive

  When a person exhibits traits expected from

aggressive and passive personalities, they may be labeled as a passive-aggressive communicator. Passivity can be observed in the way they rarely express their own needs, wants, thoughts, and feelings to others. Instead, they sneak them out in less explosive bouts of aggressiveness that others may find as underhanded or malicious.

For example, when you typically tell your dissatisfaction with your colleague's performance through ambiguous but annoying comments, typically said in a sarcastic manner, then you may be a passive-aggressive person. The intent behind such sly remarks is not to be helpful or constructive, but to subtly imply your disappointments without ever meaning to confront the other person about it. Muttering to oneself also indicates a passive-aggressive approach to resolving conflicts or issues with another person.

Common body gestures and facial expressions

associated with a passive-aggressive personality includes faking a smile when you feel upset, rolling the eyes at someone else, or sighing out. They keep their true feelings inside and let some of it out in disruptive ways that may ruin relationships or sabotage the outcome of their endeavors.

Verbal clues associated with aggressive, passive, or passive-aggressive forms of communication are likely to draw out negative feedback from those around you. Though using assertive means of communicating verbally with others may not be a total success every time, it will yield better results in the long run.

It is important to note as well that how your words are perceived may be influenced by the reputation you have built for yourself. If you have shown time and again that you have integrity and a good character, then small errors in your chosen words may be overlooked or even forgiven by those who listen to you. Otherwise, your words may be taken out of context and interpreted as rude or malicious, when you truly mean no harm by saying them.

How we describe other people and what we say about them does · not reflect their character, but ours instead. When you speak of others in a negative light, it does not only hurt the person's feelings, but it might also ruin the perception of others about you as a credible and reputable individual. Studies suggest that many people speaking negatively against others believe that it is done for one's personal gain.

This we speak ill of another person who is not present at the given moment, the chances of earning a bad reputation increases further. This effect holds true in every setting, such when you hang out with your peers or when you discuss business matters at work.

Holding back the negativity can be a hard feat for many, but it would improve your personal brand towards others. By doing so, you are exemplifying self-control and empathy—good personality traits that people value and respect. This would also improve your mood and general disposition since using negative words frequently can influence your emotions and level of stress.

There are certain occasions when you do need to speak of someone else's shortcomings and mistakes. Performance reviews, for example, will not be beneficial to the reviewee if only the good points were to be pointed out. In such instances, it is important to exercise diplomacy and tact. Avoid ad hominem arguments, wherein you attack the individual on a subjective and personal level, rather than going over the matters objectively. Use your words instead to guide the person into correcting their mistakes and improving their performance.

To further avoid the usage of negative words that could be detrimental to your personal relationships and career growth, here are some tips that may consider doing in your day-to-day life.

- Think first before speaking.

    Take a quick pause before speaking in order to assess how your words will make the other person feel. Speaking when you are feeling emotional or spiteful can lead to regrettable moments that you cannot take back. Furthermore, by choosing to quell the urge to lash out on others with your words, you are showing them that you are in control of yourself. It also denotes your concern for the wellbeing of others and exhibits a confirmation of your good personal values.

- Choose your company.

The group of people you choose to surround yourself influences you in both tangible and unnoticeable ways. When your group of friends thrive on putting down others, you may grow accustomed to such attitudes and gradually believe that is normal and acceptable behavior. In time, this will reflect on how others view your own personality. If you belong to such a group, it is time for you to reconsider your choices and make necessary adjustments in order to infuse positivity back into your social groups.

The Relationship Between Words and Personality

Words, whether spoken or written, reveal far more information than the person is intending to say in the first place. From how you choose to describe someone to how you phrase your thoughts in a social media post, words can expose your true personality and values to the interpretation of other people.

One of the most common reminders given to those who want to improve how they communicate is to "choose your words more carefully." Research shows that this is a sound advice since there is growing evidence on how revealing our words are. On a basic level, people who were identified as extraverted speak louder and use more words than introverted individuals. Their rate of speech tends to be faster as well. Speaking in a group setting is observed to be more common among women who scored highly in the extraversion scale, while introverted men tend to speak more to themselves only.

Going further, researchers found that introverted and extraverted people have different preferences when it comes to their choice of words. An experiment conducted among university students show that extraverted people prefer using abstract terms when describing other people, an object, or an idea, while their introverted counterparts use specific, concrete words. For example, an extravert might say, "This apple tastes good." On the other hand, an introvert would describe the same apple in this manner, "This apple tastes sweet and juicy."

Further results indicate the introverted people use more articles—the parts of speech that describes the noun that follows them. In the English language, there are only three articles: "a," "an", and "the". Introverts also exercise more caution and hesitation as exhibited by their choice of words. They use words that pad their original intent, making them sound less demanding than the extraverts. To illustrate this, examine these two sentences:

- "Let's head out for lunch. There's a new diner that opened just recently."

- "Perhaps we could go out for lunch and get a sandwich."

Both sentences have the same intent, but the first one is spoken by an extraverted person, while the second statement is made by an introverted person.

In terms of personality types, these findings are consistent with how people are classified based on the traits they exhibit. Extraverted people are more open to new experiences, but are less likely to be bothered by the small details than their introverted counterparts. They are more willing to take bigger risks and therefore are willing to arrive faster to decisions and commitments.

Aside from extraversion/introversion personality scale, words also denote where the person fall in terms of open-mindedness, neuroticism, and conscientiousness. For example, people who have more liberal tendencies than conservative ones use more words that pertain to their senses. Highly strung people, on the other hand, use more emotive words when they communicate with others. People concerned with their achievement are more likely to use active forms of sentences rather than passive ones.

Personality is also revealed in written words as well. Another study conducted among college students show their differences when asked to write about their previous life experiences and future career goals. The researchers observed that students with high extraversion ratings write more words referring to their relationships with other people compared to those who were identified as introverted.

Another experiment is conducted using a creative writing as a means of determining the personality of the writer. The researchers give the writers these prompt words as a basis for a short story: "Middle Ages", "fireworks", "plane crash", "supermarket", and "parlor maid". As instructed, the short story must include all five words. Results of the study indicate that writers who belong to the open-minded category produced more creative output, while those who scored low in neuroticism and conscientiousness have writer stories with themes that socializing with others.

Majority of these studies on language have examined

how people speak when they know they are being examined. When researchers observe groups of people engaged in a conversation, a new side of how words reveal our personality has been discovered. A group of introverted people began conversing about the problems and how they are attempting to solve them, while the group with extraverted people talked more about their experiences about a wide of topics. Such findings remain consistent with the how people belonging to either the introversion and extraversion categories are described in psychological terms.

Researchers have also examined online blogs and social media posts by their participants. Their observations indicate that usage of words align with the personality type of the person who posted the message or article online. For example, people who were identified as agreeable use less swear words than the neurotic bloggers and social media account users. The latter also were observed to use more frequently the singular form of personal pronouns in the first-person point of view, such as "I" and "me". Extraverted people write more about the social events had participated in and their choice of words in such posts leaned towards a more positive tone compared to all other types of personalities.

The abovementioned findings are consistent with another experiment conducted among people reading tweets posted by strangers. Most of the participants were able to guess correctly the personality type of the original poster just by merely examining the words used in the tweet. Even with the handles used for an email account, words are also used to judge the owner's personality. Studies suggest that email addresses with a relatively long string of numerical digits in them are believed to be owned by people with a more casual approach to life in general. On the other hand, email addresses that contain a humorous word or phrase are believed to be owned by extroverts. This, however, is an inaccurate judgment, proving that assessments that relied on only one factors will lead to erroneous analysis of other people's personalities.

These researches in the relationship between words and personality may cause you discomfort, especially if you prefer to keep certain information about yourself from being exposed to other people's judgment. However, knowing how powerful your words can be may be the jumping point you need to reevaluate your choice of words in order to gain more positive feedback from other people.

Conclusion

I'd like to thank you and congratulate you for transiting my lines from start to finish.

I hope this book was able to help you to learn how to observe, interpret, and understand people through their non-verbal behaviors. I also hope that you have further gained a well-rounded view of how body language interacts with verbal clues in order to create a more effective means of conveying a message to other people.

The next step is to continue practicing your newfound skill of analyzing people scientifically. You now know which verbal and non-verbal cues to look for, and how each contributes to your understanding of the thoughts, feelings, and attitudes of a person. But like the other important skills we have learned, it is important to apply this knowledge and hone your abilities every which way you can.

You may opt to observe real-life people doing their

day-to-day tasks or engaging with their peers. Pick a strategic spot where you can do so without appearing like a creep or a snoop. Observe their actions in silence and recall what you have learned from this book. Once you have become accustomed to this, noticing key gestures and facial expressions made by other people can become a natural habit for you.

Watching the television with no sound on is another method of practicing your skills at reading other people. Predict what the characters in film or television show are feeling, or how they will react in a given situation. Once you have your educated guess, turn the sound back on and see for yourself how well you did.

Copyright @2019 By Jeremiah Bonn

All Rights Reserved.

Printed in Great Britain
by Amazon